Preventing Challenging Behavior

in Your Classroom

Positive Behavior Support and Effective Classroom Management

Preventing Challenging Behavior
in Your Classroom

Positive Behavior Support and Effective Classroom Management

Matt Tincani

PRUFROCK PRESS INC.
WACO, TEXAS

Tincani, Matthew J.
  Preventing challenging behavior in your classroom : positive behavior support and effective classroom management / by Matt Tincani.
     p. cm.
  Includes bibliographical references.
  ISBN 978-1-59363-718-7 (pbk.)
  1. Classroom management. 2. Problem children--Behavior modification. I. Title.
  LB3013.T585 2011
  371.102'4--dc22

                        2011008658

Edited by Lacy Compton

Layout Design by Raquel Trevino

Author photograph reprinted with permission.
Copyright © 2011 by Gretchen Johnson Photography.

ISBN-13: 978-1-59363-718-7

Prufrock Press Inc.
P.O. Box 8813
Waco, TX 76714-8813
Phone: (800) 998-2208
Fax: (800) 240-0333
http://www.prufrock.com

Dedication

This book is dedicated to my students, who have taught me more than I could ever teach them.

Contents

Introduction

Virtually all teachers will encounter students who display problem behaviors in their classrooms. Positive behavior support (PBS) has evolved as the preeminent, research-based approach to help students with challenging behaviors to succeed in classroom settings. Educators across the country are embracing PBS as their primary means for student discipline, and a working knowledge of PBS is essential for classroom teachers to fully meet their students' learning, behavioral, and social needs, and to fulfill requirements of state and federal mandates.

Preventing Challenging Behavior in Your Classroom: Positive Behavior Support and Effective Classroom Management targets regular and special education teachers who implement PBS in their classrooms. The book also serves as an essential resource for preservice teachers who are developing their classroom management skills. It focuses on practical strategies to prevent and reduce behavior problems and enhance student learning. Initial chapters overview the conceptual and empirical basis of PBS; however, much of the book describes PBS for inclusive settings, including techniques for students with and without disabilities. PBS interventions from peer-reviewed research are highlighted in easy-to-understand language to facilitate teachers' knowledge of evidence-based techniques. Real-world examples are provided in conjunction with activities to enhance teachers' understanding and mastery of the book's content.

Chapter 1, What Is Positive Behavior Support?, presents a brief history and overview of PBS, including primary, secondary, and tertiary levels of prevention. The chapter provides a context for the book's focus on classroom-level interventions.

Chapter 2, Myths and Facts About Effective Classroom Management, describes common misconceptions about classroom management, setting the stage for a discussion of effective interventions.

Chapter 3, The Foundation: Classroom Organization, discusses the keys to good classroom organization with real-world examples of organizational techniques.

Chapter 4, Active Student Responding to Prevent Challenging Behaviors, presents instructional techniques that encourage active student responding to reduce challenging behavior in the classroom. Strategies covered in this chapter include response cards, choral responding, guided notes, and brisk instructional pacing.

Chapter 5, Classroom-Wide Behavior Support, overviews basic principles of behavior and targeted strategies for students at risk for academic failure due to behavior problems.

Chapter 6, Functional Behavioral Assessment, targets students with chronic challenging behaviors. The chapter describes why students engage in problem behaviors and presents a continuum of strategies to assess behavior functions.

Chapter 7, Function-Based Interventions and Behavior Intervention Programming, discusses strategies for individualized interventions, with an emphasis on function-based supports and behavior intervention program development.

Chapter 8, Using Data to Evaluate PBS Outcomes, overviews the role of data in program evaluation, with techniques to collect and evaluate student data.

The last section of the book, Putting It Together: The Reflective Classroom Manager Survey, presents one strategy for assessing and improving the teacher's implementation of effective classroom management techniques.

Each chapter begins with a set of chapter objectives. The reader should overview each objective to understand what he or she is expected to learn. Each chapter also contains a set of guided activities embedded throughout the text. It is useful to complete these activities while reading the text to enhance understanding of the chapters' content. Finally, the last section contains the Reflective Classroom Manager Survey, which is designed to help in-service teachers reflect on their use of techniques described in the book and to develop an action plan for improving key strategies.

CHAPTER 1

What Is Positive Behavior Support?

Chapter Objectives

- Describe the history of PBS.

- Understand how PBS is part of the IEP process in special education.

- Identify the critical features of PBS.

- Describe the three levels of PBS intervention.

- Describe the relationship between PBS and Response to Intervention.

In this chapter, we will overview the history of positive behavior support and its role within special education and behavior intervention programming. We will identify the critical features of PBS and explore school-based applications of each critical feature. Then, we will learn about primary, secondary, and tertiary prevention as core elements of PBS in schools. Finally, we will describe what PBS shares in common with Response to Intervention.

Ms. Ramirez's New Class

Ms. Ramirez is excited to begin her first year of teaching. She recently completed a teacher preparation program at a local university and has secured a position in an inclusive elementary school classroom. She is eager to organize her room, plan her lessons, and meet her students, but she is anxious about the challenges her first year of teaching will present. After reviewing her new students' *Individualized Education Programs* (IEPs), she realizes that several of them have *behavior intervention plans* (BIPs) to reduce problem behaviors. Furthermore, the students' BIPs include an unfamiliar term, *positive behavior support* (PBS). With this new information in mind, she wonders how she can best enable all of her students to be successful in school, including her students with challenging behaviors.

What Is Positive Behavior Support?

Positive Behavior Support and the IEP

As Ms. Ramirez's vignette illustrates, there is a lot of information for new teachers to learn. For instance, all students with disabilities who receive special education services have an IEP that describes their annual goals and short-term objectives, how their educational progress will be measured, and what accommodations and related services they will receive, in addition to other important information, in compliance with the Individuals with Disabilities Education Improvement Act of 2004 (IDEA). In essence, the IEP describes how a student's special education program will be delivered and the manner in which the student's educational progress will be evaluated.

Some students with disabilities engage in challenging behaviors. These behaviors make it difficult for students to benefit from instruction and may create a distracting environment for others around them. For children with disabilities who engage in challenging behaviors that interfere with learning, the IEP team must consider strategies, including PBS, to minimize those behaviors. Specifically, when developing an IEP, the team must: "In the case of a child whose behavior impedes the child's learning or that of others, consider the use of *positive behavioral interventions and supports*, and other strategies, to address that behavior" (IDEA, 2004, Sec. 300.324(a)(2)(i); emphasis added).

As members of the educational team—special education teachers, regular education teachers, parents, school psychologists, administrators, and others—develop an IEP for a student with challenging behaviors, it is critical for them to consider PBS. PBS intervention strategies may be described within a behavior intervention plan (BIP), a written plan that describes procedures to prevent and reduce a student's challenging behaviors. We will learn more about BIPs in Chapter 7.

Behavior intervention plan (BIP): A written plan that describes procedures to prevent and reduce a student's challenging behaviors, and how data will be used to evaluate these procedures. BIPs are designed for students who display chronic or intense challenging behaviors.

Individualized Education Program (IEP): A written plan that describes how a student's special education program will be delivered and evaluated. Required components include present levels of performance, measurable goals and objectives, related services and accommodations, and how the child's progress will be documented.

Positive behavior support (PBS): An approach to prevent and reduce challenging behavior through comprehensive lifestyle change, a lifespan perspective, stakeholder participation, socially valid interventions, systems change, multicomponent intervention, prevention, flexibility with respect to scientific practices, and multiple theoretical perspectives.

Positive Behavior Support and Effective Classroom Management

But there is much more to PBS than developing BIPs for students with behavior problems. As we will see, PBS includes a variety of strategies to help teachers effectively manage their classrooms to promote student learning. In fact, a central component of PBS is arranging the student's environment to *prevent* challenging behaviors from occurring to begin with (Carr et al., 2002). With this in mind, we will discuss PBS as a comprehensive approach to prevent and reduce challenging behaviors and to enhance students' overall success in school and quality of life.

Defining Positive Behavior Support

The importance of PBS to effective behavior intervention is clear; however, there is no simple, straightforward definition of PBS, nor is PBS associated exclusively with any particular set of teaching techniques. The best way to understand PBS is to examine its historical roots, defining features, and applications within school settings.

PBS emerged more than two decades ago as a movement to support the use of nonaversive behavior interventions for persons with disabilities (Horner, Dunlap, Koegel, & Carr, 1990). Until the 1990s, it was not uncommon for students to receive humiliating, painful, or physically harmful "treatments"—including physical and chemical restraints—to reduce their problem behaviors. PBS emerged in part as a movement to discourage educators from using such aversive procedures. However, the founders of PBS were careful to extend its scope beyond rejection of aversive interventions. They defined PBS to include a range of approaches that emphasized (a) effective, positive procedures; (b) social validation and human dignity; and (c) prohibition of certain aversive behavior change techniques, including those involving pain, harm, disrespect, or dehumanization (Horner et al., 1990). We will discuss specific reasons for avoiding punishment aversive behavior interventions in Chapter 2.

Importantly, the field of PBS has been heavily influenced by the science of *applied behavior analysis* (ABA; Cooper, Heron, & Heward, 2007) and shares much in common with it. For example, ABA and PBS emphasize data-based decision making, careful examination of the students' environment to understand why behaviors are occurring, and a practical, problem-solving approach to intervention (Dunlap, Carr, Horner, Zarcone, & Schwartz, 2008). Indeed, many of the procedures described throughout this book come directly from the science of ABA (Cooper et al., 2007). Yet there are several critical features of contemporary PBS that set it apart from ABA (Carr et al., 2002): (a) comprehensive lifestyle change and quality of life, (b) a lifespan perspective, (c) stakeholder participation, (d) social validity, (e) systems change and multicomponent intervention, (f) emphasis on prevention, (g) flexibility with respect to scientific practices, and (h) multiple theoretical perspectives. Each is described in the next section.

> **Applied behavior analysis (ABA):** Application of the science of behavior analysis to improve socially significant behaviors. ABA emphasizes continuous measurement, close examination of the student's environment, and manipulation of antecedents and consequences to accomplish behavior change.

Critical Features of Positive Behavior Support

The critical features of PBS are summarized below (see Carr et al., 2002, for more information on each of the critical features). Although each one is distinct, you will notice overlap among them. We will refer to the critical features of PBS throughout the remaining chapters of the book as we discuss applications of PBS in classroom management.

Comprehensive Lifestyle Change and Quality of Life

The focus of intervention is not just the problem behavior itself, but how the problem behavior affects the student's lifestyle and quality of life.

For example, Joseph, a preschool student, often hits his classmates to access a toy he wants. Joseph's hitting is not only disruptive to the classroom, but his behavior has caused other students to avoid him, and he has formed few friendships with his peers. Joseph's hitting has negatively affected his quality of life by limiting his social relationships. If PBS is successful, Joseph will not only hit his peers less frequently, but he will also have more friendships with the students in his class. We could measure this outcome by recording the frequency of appropriate, reciprocal peer interactions before and after intervention. Increased peer interactions would indicate that Joseph's quality of life has improved according to the dimension of friendships.

Lifespan Perspective

The intervention accomplishes both short- and long-term behavior change. Positive outcomes are measured not just in days and weeks, but in months and years.

For example, Elaine is a 16-year-old girl with intellectual disabilities. Upon finishing high school, she wants to secure competitive employment in the community. However, her occasional outbursts have prevented her from participating in her high school's work study program. Therefore, a short-term goal of PBS for Elaine is inclusion in her high school's work study program, and a long-term goal is attaining a full-time job when she graduates. Elaine's educational team will consider both her short- and long-term vocational goals when developing her PBS plan.

Stakeholder Participation

Stakeholders are actively involved in the design and implementation of behavior support programs. Stakeholders can include parents, grandparents, teachers, siblings, friends, or anyone who has a meaningful relationship with the focus person.

For example, Rashad's educational team convenes to develop his PBS plan. The team is comprised not only of educators and Rashad's parents, but also his grandparents and older sister. The team seeks input from each family member to identify routines in the home setting that are affected by his problem behavior. Family members help to select target behaviors and to design interventions that will reduce his challenging behaviors across settings.

Social Validity

Interventions are evaluated not only in terms of objective data, but also in terms of stakeholders' subjective perceptions of their utility and effectiveness. Team members seek active input from stakeholders on the goals of interventions, their feasibility, and how effective they are in producing desired outcomes.

For example, Julio's team implements a PBS plan to reduce his destructive and aggressive behaviors. As the plan is developed, Julio's teacher and teaching assistant are actively engaged by the team to ensure that they understand the plan and can implement it. The procedures are adjusted to meet their skills and preferences. After the plan is put in place, the team periodically evaluates the staff's satisfaction with the procedures and, importantly, whether they have continued to implement them. The teacher and teaching assistant are satisfied with the procedures and outcomes of Julio's PBS plan, and have continued to implement the plan with fidelity.

Systems Change and Multicomponent Intervention

Long-term solutions rely upon changing environments that support problem behaviors, with careful attention to the people who implement PBS. No behavior reduction program will be successful unless stakeholders understand the procedures, are well trained, and have the resources to be successful. Because the environments in which students behave are complex, successful plans must have multiple procedures to address challenging behaviors.

For example, Rollins Middle School has a high rate of office discipline referrals, detentions, and suspensions among its students. To address students' chronic behavior problems, the Rollins' staff implements a School-Wide Positive Behavior Support Program (SWPBS; Sugai & Horner, 2002), which is developed with input from the entire school staff. The program includes ongoing personnel training and data-based decision making. Multiple interventions are developed at the schoolwide, classroom, and individual student levels to address the discipline needs of all students.

Emphasis on Prevention

Well-designed behavior support plans prevent challenging behaviors. Therefore, behavior change procedures are in place when problem behaviors are not occurring, and school personnel adopt a proactive, skill-building approach to solving behavior problems.

For example, Emily is a middle school student with autism. She often becomes confused and has tantrums during activity transitions. Recognizing the need to make Emily's transitions more concrete, her teacher implements a picture activity schedule to prevent tantrums. Once in place, Emily no longer becomes confused when activities end, and she has learned to become more independent as she transitions from one activity to the next.

Flexibility With Respect to Scientific Practices and Multiple Theoretical Perspectives

The practice of PBS reflects influence of diverse scientific, theoretical, and professional perspectives. Team members recognize the role of the focus person's learning history, social systems, and cultural contexts as critical influences on his or her behavioral development. Team members value the perspectives of professionals from varying disciplines and the diverse perspectives they bring to bear on solutions to challenging behaviors.

For example, Naoki is a prekindergarten student with intellectual disabilities and challenging behaviors whose family recently emigrated from Japan. His PBS team carefully listens to his parents to understand their goals for intervention. They learn that Naoki spends much of his time with his mother and that his problem behaviors have made her and Naoki relatively isolated with few trips into the community. Therefore, the PBS team develops interventions that seek to reduce his problem behaviors within relevant community routines (e.g., grocery shopping, doctor's office). Similar interventions are applied in the school setting.

Applying PBS in Schools: School-Wide Positive Behavior Support and the PBS Triangle

The critical features of PBS have been applied in thousands of schools within a model known as School-Wide Positive Behavior Support (Horner et al., 2009; Sugai & Horner, 2002, 2008). SWPBS uses a three-tiered

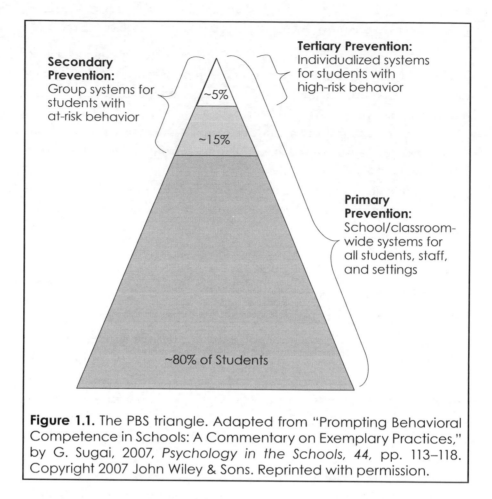

Secondary Prevention: Group systems for students with at-risk behavior

Tertiary Prevention: Individualized systems for students with high-risk behavior

~5%

~15%

Primary Prevention: School/classroom-wide systems for all students, staff, and settings

~80% of Students

Figure 1.1. The PBS triangle. Adapted from "Prompting Behavioral Competence in Schools: A Commentary on Exemplary Practices," by G. Sugai, 2007, *Psychology in the Schools, 44,* pp. 113–118. Copyright 2007 John Wiley & Sons. Reprinted with permission.

model to address problem behaviors, with a focus on prevention, stakeholder participation, systems change, and multicomponent interventions. The three-tiered model has been depicted in the PBS triangle shown in Figure 1.1. As you can see, the triangle is composed of primary, secondary, and tertiary levels of prevention. Importantly, SWPBS is a comprehensive approach that addresses students' behaviors differently based on their individual needs.

Primary Prevention

Primary prevention efforts focus on all of the students in a school, about 80% of whom require only this level of support. An important goal of these procedures is to prevent students who display low-level challenging behaviors from needing more intensive interventions. Primary prevention is comprised of universal interventions that are implemented in all school settings (e.g., classrooms, hallways, cafeteria, playground). Examples of universal interventions include schoolwide rules and expectations, procedures for teaching rules and expectations, schoolwide reward systems, and data-based monitoring.

Secondary Prevention

Secondary prevention targets students who are at risk for academic failure because of their challenging behaviors. These students comprise about 15% of the school's population. One important reason for these strategies is to prevent students who display moderate levels of problem behaviors from needing intensive, individualized interventions. Secondary prevention consists of specialized group interventions, which are often implemented at the classroom level. Examples of secondary interventions include classwide token reward systems, interventions for promoting active student responding, social skills training, and peer-mediated strategies. Examples of secondary interventions will be described in Chapters 4 and 5, Active Student Responding to Prevent Challenging Behavior and Classroom-Wide Behavior Support.

Tertiary Prevention

Tertiary prevention focuses on students with serious, chronic challenging behaviors that substantially interfere with their learning or the learning of others. The primary purpose of tertiary prevention is to reduce the effects of the student's chronic problem behaviors on her academic, social, and behavioral success. Students at the tertiary level comprise only 5% of the school's population. Often, these students receive special education services and/or require BIPs to address their problem behaviors. Tertiary interventions are intensive, individualized, and based on behavior function, that is, the antecedents and consequences that maintain problem responses. Examples of tertiary prevention are described in Chapter 7, Function-Based Intervention and Behavior Intervention Programming.

Activity

Consider a student you know who exhibits challenging behaviors, or think of a hypothetical student who exhibits challenging behaviors. Based on what you just read, provide at least one example of primary, secondary, and tertiary interventions that would be appropriate to prevent and reduce the student's problem behaviors. These could be strategies that are already in place or new strategies.

- Primary prevention: _____

    _____

    _____

    _____

    _____

    _____

    _____

- Secondary prevention: _____

    _____

    _____

    _____

    _____

    _____

    _____

- Tertiary prevention: _____

    _____

    _____

    _____

    _____

    _____

    _____

PBS and Response to Intervention

Response to Intervention (RtI) is a related approach that is gaining popularity in schools. RtI uses a multitiered prevention model to help students who are at risk for academic difficulty because of learning problems (Fuchs & Deshler, 2007; Fuchs & Fuchs, 2008). Like PBS, RtI emphasizes prevention of academic failure through proactive strategies; however, RtI focuses primarily on academic skills while PBS focuses on challenging behaviors. Nonetheless, PBS and RtI are complementary approaches.

> **Response to Intervention (RtI):** A multitiered approach that emphasizes prevention of academic failure through early screening and intervention.

One model of RtI consists of a three-tiered approach to prevent academic failure. Tier I is comprised of effective general education for all students to teach reading, math, and other fundamental academic skills. At Tier I, all students are routinely screened for the early signs of academic difficulties; those who are identified as "nonresponders"—that is, they do not display grade- or age-level proficiency with effective general education—are referred for more intensive interventions at Tier II. Students who fail to respond to interventions at Tiers I and II are evaluated for special education services and receive individual academic interventions at Tier III. An important goal of RtI is to reduce the number of students who need special education services through early screening and early intervention (Bayat, Mindes, & Covitt, 2010).

Summary

Positive behavior support emerged in the early 1990s as an alternative to aversive interventions for problem behaviors. Influenced strongly by the science of applied behavior analysis, contemporary PBS has evolved into a comprehensive approach to challenging behaviors that emphasizes: (a) comprehensive lifestyle change and quality of life; (b) a lifespan perspective; (c) stakeholder participation; (d) social validity; (e) systems change and multicomponent intervention; (f) emphasis on prevention; (g) flexibility with respect to scientific practices; and (h) multiple theoretical perspectives. PBS is embedded within IDEA 2004; professionals must employ PBS strategies with students who have disabilities and display problem behaviors that interfere with their instruction or the instruction of others. PBS has been widely implemented in an approach know as School-Wide Positive Behavior Support, which is guided by three levels of prevention: primary, secondary, and tertiary. Response to Intervention is a related approach that emphasizes prevention of academic failure through a multitiered screening and an intervention process.

Chapter Resources

To learn more about PBS and RtI, visit the following websites:
- Association for Positive Behavior Support: http://www.apbs.org
- Technical Assistance Center on Positive Behavioral Interventions and Supports: http://www.pbis.org
- Technical Assistance Center on Social Emotional Intervention for Young Children: http://www.challengingbehavior.org
- National Center on Response to Intervention: http://www.rti4success.org

CHAPTER 2

Myths and Facts About Effective Classroom Management

Chapter Objectives

♦ Understand the Creative Teacher Myth and how to be a critical consumer of classroom management strategies.

♦ Describe the Bad Student Myth and the role of alterable variables in positive behavior support.

♦ Explain the Rewards Myth and why rewards are critical to successful classroom management.

♦ Understand the Punishment Myth and the reasons why punishment should be avoided as a classroom management technique.

In this chapter you will learn about four myths of effective classroom management: the Creative Teacher Myth, the Bad Student Myth, the Rewards Myth, and the Punishment Myth. We will also explore facts about effective classroom management and how these play a key role in your success as a classroom teacher.

The Creative Teacher Myth

Myth: Creativity is the key to successful classroom management.
Fact: Effective classroom management is not determined by creativity, but by how skillfully the teacher applies systematic, data-based management strategies in the classroom.

Consider this unfortunate scenario. You fall from a ladder and hurt your ankle. It is painful and difficult to walk. Suspecting a broken bone, you visit the emergency room. The doctor examines your ankle and without taking an x-ray prescribes a surprising treatment. "I've never tried this before. I heard that if you rub this cream on your skin it can heal broken bones. It might help with your ankle." Shocked, you ask what the cream has to do with healing fractures. "I'm not sure, but it sounds like a good idea and it could work." You leave the ER in disbelief, wondering how a doctor could practice medicine in such an unsystematic way.

It is hard to imagine being treated this way by a physician, but many teachers adopt a similar approach to classroom management. When confronted with student behavior problems, they utilize creative, yet ineffective strategies to fix them. Educators who use invented classroom management strategies fail to realize that although virtually any strategy *could* work, those that are based on data and sound research are much more likely to work than those produced by intuition, instinct, and creativity. The field of medicine has been guided by scientifically based practice for many decades. In contrast, the profession of teaching has yet to fully embrace research-based instructional and classroom management practices.

Teachers cannot be faulted for poor classroom management. In one survey, more than 40% reported that problem behaviors interfered with their teaching (National Center for Education Statistics, 2000), and student misbehavior is consistently associated with higher levels of teacher stress and burnout (Clunies-Ross, Little, & Kienhuis, 2008; Keiper & Busselle, 1996; Kokkinos, 2007; Lewis, 1999). Despite the problems associated with challenging behaviors, many teachers report feeling underprepared to manage their classrooms (National Center for Educational Statistics, 1999). Teachers' lack of preparedness in classroom management can be traced in part to college and university preparation programs. In a 2009 speech, Arne Duncan, U.S. Secretary of Education, criticized teacher preparation programs for failing to provide teachers with "hands-on practical . . . training about managing the classroom" and strategies on "how to use data to differentiate and improve instruction and boost student learning." His criticisms echo concerns expressed by educators about widespread myths of teaching; for example, that good teachers are simply born that way (Snider, 2006) or that structured curricula and learning objectives impede student learning (Heward, 2003). Sadly, these longstanding myths not only inhibit teachers' effectiveness as classroom managers, but they also contribute to marginal test scores, academic failure, drop-out, and other poor outcomes among our students, particularly those who are considered "hard to teach."

Fortunately, the fact that you, a current or future teacher, are reading this book attests to your willingness to adopt a more effective approach to classroom management. A rich collection of literature with effective strategies from the field of PBS exists to help you (Simonsen, Fairbanks, Briesch, Myers, & Sugai, 2008). School-Wide Positive Behavior Support, a systematic approach to school discipline and classroom management, has been empirically tested in thousands of schools across the U.S. (Horner et al., 2009; Sugai, 2007; see Chapter 1). The success of SWPBS highlights the importance of systematic, data-based approaches to effective behavior management.

The first step to becoming an effective classroom manager is to be a critical consumer of classroom management approaches. The following questions can guide you when presented with a potential classroom management strategy (see also Heward, 2003).

- Does the strategy offer an easy fix or magic bullet to solve the problem? If yes, be skeptical.
- Is the strategy supported by research published in peer-reviewed journals?
- Has the strategy been empirically tested in real classrooms with teachers implementing it?
- Does the strategy employ data to evaluate student outcomes? How?

The Bad Student Myth

Myth: Some students are just bad and there isn't anything the teacher can do about it.

Fact: Teachers can improve virtually all students' behavior and learning.

I teach a behavior management course to beginning teachers. At the beginning of each semester, I pose the following question to the class: "Why do students misbehave?" Their answers usually fall into two categories. The first is comprised of responses such as, "Because class is boring," or "Their behavior gets the teacher's attention," or "The work is too difficult." The second consists of answers like "a disability," or "bad genes," or "poverty." What is the difference between them? The first category is comprised of responses that refer to *alterable variables*, or things that the teacher can control to alter student learning and behavior (Bloom, 1980; Heward, 2003). For example, the teacher can change her pace of teaching, her responses to problem behaviors, or provide a choice of materials to make class less boring and less likely to trigger student misbehavior. The second refers to *nonalterable variables*, or things that are beyond the teacher's control. For instance, a student's disability or his genes are not something the teacher can change. Other examples are found in Table 2.1.

> **Alterable variables:** Things the teacher can change to produce improvements in students' learning and behaviors. These include the pace of teaching, responses to problem behaviors, and choice of materials.
>
> **Nonalterable variables:** Things that affect students' learning and behaviors that are beyond the teacher's control. Some examples include disabilities, genes, and poverty.

I conduct this question-and-answer activity to draw attention to the Bad Student Myth, that is, due to a variety of reasons—such as disability, intelligence, genes, poverty, or parents—the student will engage in challenging behaviors and there is little the teacher can do about it. Although it is true that these factors influence students' behaviors, they do not necessarily overshadow the effects of good teaching and classroom management. Furthermore, because the teacher's role is to provide good instruction, it is much more productive to focus on the things that you can control—that is, your teaching—than to blame students' challenging behaviors on things beyond your influence.

A common example of the Bad Student Myth occurs when we attribute a student's challenging behaviors to his disability. For example, when a student with autism engages in problem behaviors such as

Table 2.1
Examples of Alterable and Nonalterable Variables

Alterable Variables	Nonalterable Variables
Pace of instruction	Student's disability
Choices in the classroom	Student's community (e.g., poverty, crime)
Responses to student problem behaviors	Student's parents
Use of rewards or praise	Student's genes
Activity schedules	Student's personality
Curriculum materials	School administrators
Opportunities for active student responding	Past teachers who didn't do their job

tantrums, I've heard the following explanation: "He does that because he has autism." Although it is true that students with autism are more prone to engage in certain problem behaviors, these behaviors are often triggered by events in the classroom (e.g., an unstructured schedule) or maintained by specific consequences (e.g., escape from a nonpreferred activity). A more useful strategy is to change the classroom environment in ways that will make it unnecessary for the student to engage in such challenging behaviors.

A case study on the application of PBS with Tom, a nonverbal 2-year-old with suspected autism who engaged in tantrums (Dunlap & Fox, 1999), illustrated the value of changing alterable variables. Tom's team implemented a multicomponent intervention that included changing his environment to increase predictability, developing consistent expectations across care providers, providing a visual activity schedule, and teaching him to make choices. Figure 2.1 shows how the multicomponent intervention substantially reduced Tom's tantrums across home and childcare settings compared to the baseline. Although every child's needs are different, many can be helped with similar multicomponent strategies.

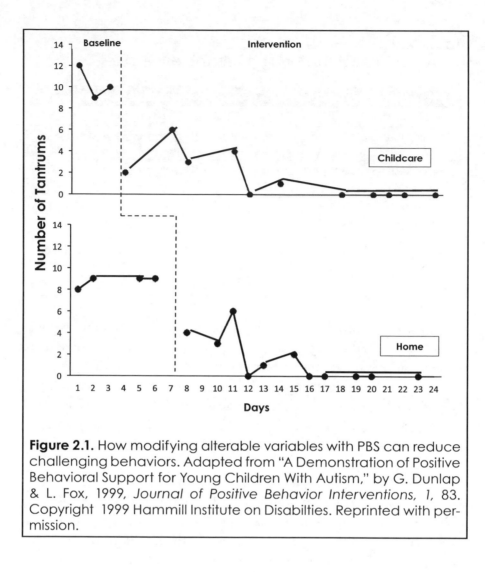

Figure 2.1. How modifying alterable variables with PBS can reduce challenging behaviors. Adapted from "A Demonstration of Positive Behavioral Support for Young Children With Autism," by G. Dunlap & L. Fox, 1999, *Journal of Positive Behavior Interventions, 1,* 83. Copyright 1999 Hammill Institute on Disabilties. Reprinted with permission.

Activity

Consider a student you know who exhibits challenging behaviors, or think of a hypothetical student who exhibits challenging behaviors. What are some ways you could lessen the child's challenging behaviors by changing the classroom environment? As you think about your answer, consider the alterable variables found in Figure 2.1.

_____

_____

_____

_____

_____

_____

_____

_____

_____

_____

_____

_____

_____

_____

_____

_____

_____

The Rewards Myth

> **Myth**: Rewards and praise undermine students' intrinsic motivation.
> **Fact**: Rewards and praise are both beneficial and necessary to effective classroom management.

Another widespread myth in education involves the teacher's use of rewards and praise. It is argued that rewards and praise undermine intrinsic motivation, foster dependence, and ultimately make students less likely to perform the behaviors that teachers are trying to teach. The best-known proponent of this view is the lecturer and author Alfie Kohn, whose anti-reward sentiments have been reflected in classroom management books and texts on student motivation. We will examine how two primary criticisms of rewards and praise are unfounded. These criticisms are that rewards and praise are (a) coercive and (b) don't work in improving students' classroom performance. In contrast, we will explore reasons that rewards and praise are critical to effective classroom management.

Rewards and Praise Are Coercive

A central tenant of the anti-rewards argument is that use of rewards, praise, grades, or any attempt to change students' behaviors through consequences is tantamount to coercion because it means we are controlling students (Kohn, 1993). Accordingly, rewarding a student is just as bad as punishing him because we are withholding something favorable if he does not perform in a prescribed manner. Instead, it is argued, students should be provided with engaging materials, choices, and encouragement to discover the correct answers in an environment free of contingencies for performance.

This perspective holds a degree of logic. In an ideal world, students should want to learn for the sake of learning without the need for incentives. Unfortunately, choices, encouragement, and discovery learning are insufficient classroom management tools for a couple of important reasons. First, consequences such as rewards (or, technically, reinforcement) and punishment are principles of human behavior that operate in the classroom irrespective of the teacher's management techniques (see Chapter 5; Cooper et al., 2007; Maag, 2001). Students will always do things to produce consequences, whether it's attention from a teacher, approval from a parent, or recognition from their peers. Rewards in the broader sense don't go away because teachers stop using reward systems—like gravity, they are just there. Teachers who fail to use rewards and praise systematically risk inadvertently reinforcing students' challenging behaviors. For example, a preschool student who needs help with her scissors discovers that screaming loudly is an effective way to get the teacher's attention. A more practical and productive approach is to capitalize on rewards and praise to prevent challenging behaviors. In this case, we could teach the student an alternative, appropriate way to get the teacher's attention (e.g., by raising her hand) and reward her for performing this alternative response. We will learn specific strategies for using praise and rewards to teach alternative behaviors in the following chapters.

Second, rewards and punishment are not equal outcomes in any sense. Virtually anyone would choose to be rewarded for doing something good than to be punished for doing something bad. There is overwhelming evidence to suggest that reward systems enhance students' motivation and engagement when used appropriately; in a meta-analysis of 101 studies, Cameron and Pierce (1994) found that, overall, praise increased students' intrinsic motivation to engage in tasks. Praise only had a negative effect on intrinsic motivation when it was applied without regard to the quality of students' performance. In contrast, punishment-based discipline systems, all too common in schools, result in higher rates of problem behaviors and lowered academic achievement (Horner et al., 2009; Sugai & Horner, 2002). In the absence of rewards and praise, students may discover what to do, but in many cases they may discover how to do something bad.

Rewards and Praise Don't Work

Another argument against using rewards and praise is that they don't work. It is argued that rewards and praise may temporarily increase student compliance, but they also foster dependence and, when withdrawn, students lose their desire to perform (Kohn, 1993). Again, this argument possesses some logic—we do not want students to depend on feedback every time they perform a response.

The question is not whether rewards work—they certainly do; however, research suggests that rewards are effective only if they are applied according to specific guidelines. For instance, Cameron and Pierce (1994) found that praise and feedback increased students' intrinsic motivation only when applied after students met a specific standard of performance. So it is important for teachers to recognize and reward both the *quality* and *accuracy* of students' responses. The concept of *thinning the schedule of reinforcement* is also critical to using rewards and praise effectively (Cooper et al., 2007). When initially teaching a skill, you should apply

Thinning the schedule of reinforcement: The process of gradually decreasing how frequently you deliver reinforcement (e.g., praise, rewards) to a student. This can be accomplished by increasing the number of responses required to earn reinforcement or by increasing the amount of time with appropriate behavior that must pass before the student earns reinforcement.

praise and feedback more frequently, perhaps after every response or every other response, on average. Then, you should gradually thin the schedule of reinforcement, so that you give praise and feedback after every third response, every fifth response, every 10th response, and so forth. In this manner, students lose their dependency on rewards and require feedback only occasionally to maintain their skills. How quickly you thin the schedule of reinforcement depends on the student and the skill.

In 1987, Lovaas reported a study on the outcome of early intensive behavioral intervention on young children with autism. His approach involved a highly intensive method of teaching emphasizing repeated practice and rewards for appropriate responding. Participants were divided into three groups, one that received intensive therapy for 40 or more hours per week, one that received intensive therapy for 10 hours per week, and another that received no therapy. The intensive therapy group made significantly more progress compared to the other groups. Almost 50% of the children in this group successfully completed first grade in the regular education classroom. Lovaas's study is one of many showing that the systematic application of rewards leads to less use of rewards and inclusion in typical educational environments.

The Punishment Myth

Myth: Students with challenging behaviors need strict discipline, including punishment.
Fact: Punishment can worsen challenging behaviors.

The final myth of classroom management is that students who display problem behaviors need stern discipline and punishment. It is hard to say how this myth originated—the concept of punishment is deeply embedded in both our culture generally and in the field of education specifically. Maag (2001) offered several reasons why teachers rely heavily on reprimands, detentions, suspensions, and expulsions to control students' behaviors. First, these procedures tend to produce immediate, if temporary, cessations in problem responses. For instance, the student who misbehaves and is sent to detention is no longer irritating to the teacher (or other students). Second, punishment—or the threat of punishment—is

Activity

Imagine that you are a teacher who is beginning a new a reward system with a group of your students. After sending a note home to inform parents about the new system, you receive a phone call from one parent who expresses concerns about the use of rewards with his daughter. Specifically, he is worried that she will no longer be motivated to do her work on her own, unless someone offers her treats, gold stars, and other classroom incentives. How would you respond to his concerns and convince him that a reward system is appropriate and useful for his child?

_____

_____

_____

_____

_____

_____

_____

_____

_____

_____

_____

_____

_____

_____

_____

_____

_____

effective for many students who display low rates of problem behaviors and comprise the majority of the school's population. Third, educators have largely ignored the data supporting the use of positive techniques (e.g., Cameron & Pierce, 1994), perhaps as a function of myths about rewards perpetuated by Kohn (1993) and others.

Punishment should be used sparingly for two important reasons. First, because punishment tends to produce immediate cessation of students' problem behaviors, teachers may be tempted to overrely on punishment techniques in the classroom. When overused, punishment leads to undesirable side effects; for example, students will avoid the people and environments where punishment occurs, or will engage in aggressive or disruptive responses toward the person administering punishment (Lee & Axelrod, 2005). Second, techniques such as detention and time-out that are intended to reduce problem behaviors often result in the opposite effect (Maag, 2001). Consider the student who dislikes math, makes abusive comments to his classmates during class, and is sent by the teacher to in-school detention. Sending the student to detention may actually reinforce inappropriate comments by allowing the student to escape from math class. Too often, punishment procedures are applied in this fashion without regard to the function of problem behaviors (see Chapter 6). In contrast, because positive behavior support techniques lack the side effects associated with punishment, they should always be a teacher's first choice when considering behavior management strategies. We will explore considerations for using positive behavior support techniques throughout the remainder of the book.

Summary

There are four myths of effective classroom management. The first myth is that creativity is the key to successful classroom management. This myth is false because good classroom managers rely less on creativity and more on empirically supported strategies to foster student success. The second is that some students are just bad and there is little the teacher can do about it. This myth is false because the teacher can improve most students' behaviors by addressing alterable variables. The third myth is that rewards don't work to improve students' performance. This myth is false because research shows that praise and rewards, when applied correctly, do improve students' learning and behavior. The final myth is that punishment is necessary for good classroom management. This myth is false because punishment is often overused and can lead to undesirable side effects. Instead, teachers should rely on positive techniques when possible.

CHAPTER 3

The Foundation: Classroom Organization

Chapter Objectives

♦ Describe how consistency and planning are critical to preventing challenging behaviors.

♦ Identify the guidelines for developing student schedules.

♦ Recognize the characteristics of whole-class and individual student schedules and considerations for designing each.

♦ Explain how to effectively organize the physical space of your classroom.

♦ Describe the qualities of efficient activity transitions.

♦ Identify strategies for effectively working with teaching assistants.

In this chapter, we will focus on the foundation of effective management—classroom organization. Organizing your classroom requires an initial investment of time and effort; however, it pays off by lessening the amount of time you spend managing students' behaviors. You will learn how organizing schedules, the physical space of your classroom, student groupings, and working effectively with teaching assistants can improve your students' independence and knowledge of the classroom routine.

Student Schedules

Consistency and Planning Are Key

Remember that a critical feature of PBS is arranging the classroom environment to *prevent* challenging behaviors (see Chapter 1). As a rule, students perform fewer challenging behaviors and are more engaged when the classroom schedule is structured and consistent (Morrison, 1979). A consistent schedule familiarizes students with the routine and helps to communicate your expectations for their performance. A consistent schedule means that activities start and stop at the same time each day and occur in a predictable, predetermined sequence to the greatest extent possible.

It is equally important to ensure that all of your instructional time is planned. For example, if students finish an independent seatwork assignment early, is there a specific activity for them to work on for the remainder of the period? Unplanned downtime gives students the opportunity to misbehave. In contrast, creating schedules helps to ensure that all of your students' instructional time is carefully arranged.

Guidelines for Developing Student Schedules

Consider the following guidelines as you develop your students' schedules.

Alternate demanding and preferred activities. Some classroom activities are more demanding than others. For instance, a math lesson is more likely to evoke student frustration than an activity comprised of free time on the computer. One way to prevent challenging behaviors is to arrange the schedule so that you alternate demanding and preferred activities. In one study, O'Reilly, Sigafoos, Lancioni, Edrisinha, and Andrews (2005) found that a schedule of alternating demanding activities with play decreased self-injurious behaviors and increased task engagement of a boy with autism. In contrast, a schedule comprised of

Consecutive Demanding Activities	Demanding and Preferred Activities Interspersed
Reading	Reading
Social Studies	Computer time
Math	Social Studies
Computer time	Free play
Break	Math
Free play	Break
Lunch	Lunch

Figure 3.1. Two student schedules. The left schedule has demanding activities ordered consecutively. The right schedule has demanding and preferred activities interspersed.

several consecutive, demanding activities produced frustration and consequently triggered problem behaviors. Figure 3.1 shows two schedules. The one on the left consists of demanding activities ordered consecutively. The one on the right is revised so that demanding and preferred activities are alternated.

Break up long activities. Even a preferred activity can become boring if it lasts for too long. Consider breaking up lengthy activities to increase student engagement. For example, if your English period lasts for 45 minutes and you assign a vocabulary activity, you could have students work independently for 20 minutes, exchange papers with a partner to correct their work for 15 minutes, and then review the correct answers as a whole class for 10 minutes. Breaking up activities in this manner adds variety and decreases the likelihood of boredom and problem behaviors.

Offer choices. *Choice making* allows students to access reinforcing items and activities through appropriate behaviors, and helps students to become self-determined learners (Wood, Fowler, Uphold, & Test, 2005). There are many ways to incorporate choice into the daily classroom routine. For instance, you can allow students to choose the location in the classroom where they work, the materials they use, the order in which they complete assignments, or the partner they work with. Importantly, you should offer *limited choices* rather than *open-ended*

Choice making: Providing students with an opportunity to make limited and reasonable choices in the context of classroom routines to promote self-determination and prosocial behaviors.

choices. For instance, you should give students a choice of two specific locations in the classroom to work rather than just letting them work anywhere they choose.

Whole-Class Schedules

Whole-class schedule: A publicly posted schedule that depicts what the entire class is doing throughout the entire school day.

A *whole-class schedule* defines what the entire class is going to be doing for the school day. Typically, the whole-class schedule aligns with the day's instructional periods (e.g., Period 1: Math, Period 2: Life Skills, Period 3: Reading). Creating a whole-class schedule is fairly straightforward; however, there are two important considerations as you develop the schedule. First, the whole-class schedule should be prominently posted and clearly readable to students and adults in the classroom. Therefore, the lettering of the schedule should be large enough for everyone to read, and it should be placed in a highly visible location (e.g., in the front of the room).

Second, it is helpful if the schedule can be revised to accommodate any changes in the daily routine, such as assemblies, standardized testing, or early dismissals. Writing the schedule on the classroom's dry erase board, as shown in Figure 3.2, enables you to make these revisions to accommodate any changes in the daily routine.

Importantly, at the beginning of the school year you should introduce the whole-class schedule to your students by verbally reviewing the day's planned activities before the first period. As students learn the routine, you can revisit the schedule to remind students about the day's activities along with any anticipated changes. A clear, prominently posted schedule serves as a visual reminder for students about the day's activities and is an integral component of a highly organized classroom.

Individual Student Schedules

Some students need personalized schedules to help them learn the daily routine. Like whole-class schedules, *individual student schedules* prevent challenging behaviors by making the classroom routine structured and predictable (Hall, McClannahan, & Krantz, 1995; Massey & Wheeler, 2000; Spriggs, Gast, & Ayres, 2007). Individual student schedules are not unlike the pocket calendars or smart phones that adults use to organize themselves. They can be both

Individual student schedule: A personalized written or pictorial schedule that lists the activities a student is supposed to do throughout the school day.

Preventing Challenging Behavior in Your Classroom

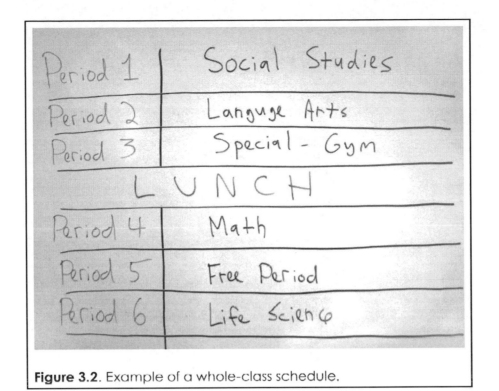

Period 1	Social Studies
Period 2	Language Arts
Period 3	Special - Gym
	LUNCH
Period 4	Math
Period 5	Free Period
Period 6	Life Science

Figure 3.2. Example of a whole-class schedule.

written and pictorial. Figures 3.3 and 3.4 show examples of written and pictorial student schedules.

Which students need activity schedules? Virtually all students benefit from some type of individualized organizational system. Secondary students can use the same types of calendars and schedules that adults use. Younger students and students with intellectual disabilities may require simplified schedules such as the ones shown in Figures 3.3 and 3.4. If the student can read, the schedule should be written at the students' reading level. If the student cannot read, then a pictorial schedule is the best choice.

There are a few guidelines to consider as you develop individual student schedules. First, when possible, it is important to involve the student in creating the schedule. For secondary students, this could mean allowing them to select the type and order of activities for the day. For younger students or students with intellectual disabilities, this could mean selecting one or two points in the schedule to provide a choice between activities. Remember that it is best to provide a limited choice between two or three activities rather than to provide an open-ended choice.

The schedule should be reviewed in advance to give students a heads up about the order of activities for the day. This could be accomplished by having the student write out the schedule before first period or, if the student is using a pictorial schedule, assisting the student in setting up

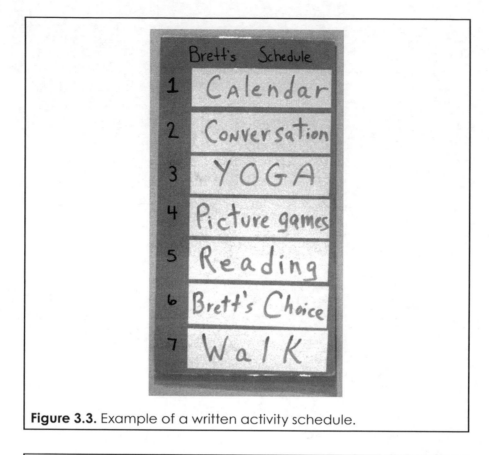

Figure 3.3. Example of a written activity schedule.

Figure 3.4. Example of a pictorial activity schedule.

the day's schedule by putting the picture symbols in the correct sequence. Similarly, you should preview any anticipated changes at the beginning of the day. For instance, if there is a special assembly during third period, homeroom is an excellent opportunity to draw the child's attention to this special event.

Activity

Imagine that it is the beginning of the school year and you are developing whole-class and individual activity schedules for your students. Make a hypothetical whole-class activity schedule for your classroom incorporating the considerations we have discussed. Then, design an individual activity schedule for a student with or without a disability that will lessen the likelihood of challenging behaviors.

Organized Physical Space

The physical space of your classroom, including desk arrangements, also affects students' success (Rosenfield, Lambert, & Black, 1985; Wannarka & Ruhl, 2008). A neat classroom with organized shelves, clearly posted schedules, and recent samples of student work creates an environment for learning. In contrast, a messy or disorganized classroom with unclear physical boundaries communicates lowered expectations to your students. Consider the following guidelines as you organize the physical space of your classroom.

Clearly Defined Instructional Areas

The physical spaces of your classroom should be organized into clearly defined instructional areas. For example, the materials for reading, language arts, social studies, and math lessons should be in separate places within the classroom. Shelves and centers should have clear visual boundaries and cues to reflect their respective purposes. These could include colored tape (e.g., red for reading vs. blue for math), picture symbols, and written signs. As with schedules, clearly defined instructional areas establish consistency and help students to learn the classroom routine.

It is also beneficial to create places in the classroom where students can turn in assignments and gather instructional materials. For instance, placing a folder for homework near the classroom door enables students to drop off completed assignments as they enter the classroom. Similarly, creating folders and shelves for students to gather specific lesson materials (e.g., worksheets, workbooks, pencils, markers) helps them to become more independent and frees the teacher from having to distribute materials during transitions and lessons.

Seating Arrangements

Student seating arrangements will vary depending on the nature of your students and the classroom activity. Low-achieving students who display challenging behaviors may benefit from sitting closer to the teacher or in the front of the room (Heron & Harris, 2001). In contrast, students who work well independently can be placed farther from the teacher and instructional stimuli.

Desks should be positioned strategically to accommodate specific activities and students. For example, if students are working on a cooperative group activity, desks can be arranged in clusters to facilitate dialogue and sharing of ideas (Heron, Hippler, & Tincani, 2003). The traditional row pattern of desks is best suited for individual student work, while the horseshoe pattern can facilitate discussion during whole-class activities (Wannarka & Ruhl, 2008). Do not be afraid to change desk or seating arrangements in order to facilitate cooperate learning and prosocial behaviors.

Traffic Patterns and Student Distractibility

It is important to think about how traffic patterns in your room will influence students' concentration as they work. For instance, if children frequently transition in and out of your classroom during instructional periods, it is a good idea to position distractible students away from the classroom door. Likewise, if there is an area of your classroom that might draw students' attention from their work (e.g., computer or free play area), it makes sense to position students who are easily distracted away from it.

Students With Physical Disabilities

Students with physical disabilities, particularly those with impairments that limit mobility, require special consideration as you arrange your classroom. Students who use wheelchairs or other assistive devices will need ample space to move around the room. The following questions bear consideration:

- Are entranceways, the spaces in between desks, and the spaces in front of shelves wide enough for students with limited mobility to navigate?
- Are instructional materials placed in close proximity so that students do not have to move across the classroom to access them?
- Are instructional materials placed on shelves so that they are in arms' reach?

Efficient Activity Transitions

Orderly activity transitions are critical to good classroom management. It is important that transitions are as brief as possible; they should be just long enough for students to move from one area of the room to another, to gather instructional materials, and then begin the lesson. Two to three minutes should be a sufficient interval for an organized transition within your classroom. A clear cue to signal the end of one activity and the beginning of the next is helpful to facilitate brief transitions. Some teachers use visual and auditory devices such as electronic timers as cues for transitions. These cues have an additional benefit of

Activity

You are rearranging the physical space of your classroom to better accommodate students with and without disabilities. Draw a map of your classroom depicting how instructional areas (e.g., student desks), your desk, storage, shelves, instructional materials, and other items will be arranged. Consider how you will organize your classroom to maximize students' attention to instruction and ability to move around and access instructional materials in a distraction-free manner.

providing feedback to students about how much time they have left to complete an activity.

Transitions will be smoother if your lesson preparation has been completed *before* the lesson begins. This means that textbooks, worksheets, and other lesson materials are ready when the activity starts. If you are still prepping as your lesson begins, this will create additional down time and will provide the opportunity for students to misbehave.

Effectively Working With Teaching Assistants

In Chapter 1, we learned that PBS interventions emphasize stakeholder participation. As members of the educational team, teaching assistants are critical stakeholders in your students' academic success and can help you create an organized classroom environment. For example, teaching assistants can assist with lesson preparation, can provide praise and rewards for students' appropriate behaviors, and can help students who need individualized assistance with classroom assignments. The following guidelines will help you to maximize the effectiveness of your teaching assistants.

- *Make your performance expectations explicit.* Teaching assistants will be more helpful if you clearly communicate your expectations for their role. One way to accomplish this is to create a schedule that delineates what you will do, as the teacher, and what the teaching assistants will do throughout the day. For instance, as you are finishing one lesson, the teaching assistant(s) can prepare materials for the next. This will facilitate smooth, brief transitions. Or, as you are delivering the lesson to the whole group, the teaching assistant(s) can provide individualized help to specific students who need it. Just like student activity schedules, teacher and teaching assistant activity schedules should be written and posted or made easily available to staff in the classroom.
- *Provide ongoing feedback.* It is important to communicate with your teaching assistants at least once per week about their performance. Weekly scheduled team meetings are a convenient time to discuss staff performance. If you must provide corrective feedback, be sure to identify at least one positive aspect of their performance to praise.

Summary

Classroom organization is critical to preventing challenging behaviors. Organization and planning are key aspects of effective classroom management. Students benefit from both whole-class and individual student activity schedules. Whole-class schedules should be clearly posted, reviewed with students, and revised as appropriate. Individual student schedules can be written or pictorial and can be used to promote choice making. Organizing the physical space of your classroom means having clearly defined instructional areas and desk arrangements that promote on-task behaviors and learning. Your classroom should also be arranged to promote the mobility of students with physical disabilities. Effective activity transitions are brief, with a clear signal to cue the beginning and end of activities. Finally, when working with teaching assistants, you should make your expectations for their performance explicit and provide ongoing feedback.

CHAPTER 4

Active Student Responding to Prevent Challenging Behaviors

Chapter Objectives

- Define active student responding (ASR).

- Describe how ASR is critical to preventing students' challenging behaviors during instruction.

- Recognize how to use response cards, choral responding, and guided notes to promote high rates of ASR.

- Identify how brisk instructional pacing increases ASR.

This chapter will focus on how teachers can promote high rates of active student responding to prevent challenging behaviors and enhance academic success. First, we will define active student responding and discuss how it is essential to good classroom management and instruction. Then, we will explore strategies for promoting active student responding. The strategies are response cards, choral responding, guided notes, and brisk instructional pacing.

What Is Active Student Responding?

Imagine that you are visiting a school to observe a fourth-grade social studies class. The teacher stands at the front of the room while asking questions about the week's lesson topic, China. A few students eagerly attend to the teacher and raise their hands each time he asks a question. Others seem less interested and occasionally raise their hands to offer an answer. About a third of the class looks bored, seldom participates, and several students are talking to their neighbors, laughing, and engaging in other off-task behaviors.

You move to another classroom and notice that students have dry erase boards on their desks. This teacher is delivering a similar lesson, but her students are much more engaged. Each time she asks a question, students quickly write answers on their dry erase boards and raise the boards to reveal their answers. All of the students in this lively classroom are responding, and you see very few off-task behaviors among the group.

> **Active student responding:** When a student emits a detectable response to ongoing instruction, such as saying, writing, or typing an answer.

The difference between the first and second classrooms illustrates the value of *active student responding* (ASR). According to Heward (1994), "ASR occurs when a student emits a detectable response to ongoing instruction" (p. 286). Examples of ASR include saying answers to teacher-posed questions, writing answers to math problems, or typing responses on a keyboard. ASR can be contrasted with unobservable or passive student responding. For example, a teacher presents a lesson and students "think" or "reflect" on their answers, or they observe other students respond, but they do not themselves perform observable responses.

Some instructional strategies are better at producing high rates of ASR than others. For instance, a teacher who presents math problems and asks students to answer by raising their hands is likely to have low rates of ASR because students can only respond one at a time. In contrast, a teacher who briskly presents math problems and then asks all students to respond by writing their answers on dry erase boards will have much higher rates of ASR and overall participation.

Why is ASR critical to good classroom management and teaching? There are two important reasons. First, the more students are actively engaged during instruction, the more likely they are to learn the curriculum, regardless of content (Greenwood, Delquadri, & Hall, 1984). Second, increasing students' rates of ASR decreases off-task behavior (Lambert, Cartledge, Heward, & Lo, 2006; Tincani & Crozier, 2007). Simply put, the more students emit active responses, the less opportunity they have to engage in disruptive behaviors. High rates of ASR produce appropriate behaviors that are incompatible with challenging behaviors.

Promoting Active Student Responding

You will learn four strategies for increasing ASR in the classroom: response cards, choral responding, guided notes, and brisk instructional pacing. Importantly, each of these strategies can be used regardless of the subject area or curriculum.

Response Cards

The vignette at the beginning of this chapter illustrates one strategy for promoting ASR: *response cards* (Heward, 1994; Lambert et al., 2006). Students either write their answers on their response cards or, if the cards are preprinted, select the correct answer from an array. Figure 4.1 shows write-on response cards, and Figure 4.2 shows preprinted response cards.

Response cards: Blank or preprinted cards on which students write or select answers during teacher directed lessons.

Response cards can be made inexpensively. The most cost-effective way to make writeon response cards is to visit your local home improvement store and purchase a sheet of bathroom board, which is used to line showers and bathtubs. It is often found in the lumber section of the store. Most home improvement stores will cut the boards into 8.5" x 11" pieces for you to create a set of individual response cards for your class. The bathroom board surface is completely erasable when used with a dry erase marker. This type of response card is shown in Figure 4.1.

Preprinted response cards can be made by laminating sheets of paper as shown in Figure 4.2. Typically, students use an object, such as a clothespin, to select the correct answer. Both true/false and multiple-choice responses can be made on preprinted response cards. For instance,

Figure 4.1. Write-on response cards.

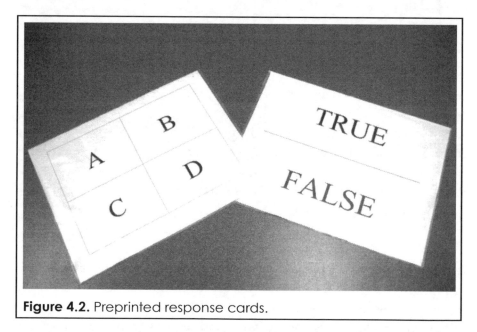

Figure 4.2. Preprinted response cards.

Godfrey, Grisham-Brown, Schuster, and Hemmeter (2003) conducted a study in which they asked preschool students "What season?" and the students selected fall, winter, spring, or summer on a preprinted response card. Preprinted response cards are ideal for younger students or for students who lack sufficient writing proficiency to use write-on response cards.

Response cards can be used across a variety of lesson content. For instance, a math teacher can present addition facts to students who can write the correct sums on their cards. A U.S. history teacher can state major events during the American Revolution and ask students to write the correct year or location. A reading teacher can say vocabulary words and have students spell the words on their cards.

Figure 4.3 shows how a typical lesson is taught using response cards (see also Heward, 1994). First, you will need to identify a set of questions, such as math facts, history facts, or vocabulary words. It is a good idea to come up with at least 10–20 questions for each lesson. If you are using write-on response cards, the answers must be short enough to fit on the response cards. Then, you will present each question to the class, as you see on the left-hand side of Figure 4.3. Visual aids, including problems written on the white board, are often helpful.

After you ask your question, allow students *wait-time* to think about and write answers on their response cards. The wait-time period should be as brief as possible (i.e., 5 seconds or less); however, difficult or new items may require additional wait-time (Tincani & Crozier, 2007). Following wait-time, you will present a cue for students to raise their cards

> **Wait-time:** The interval between when the teacher asks a question and the student responds, usually controlled by a cue from the teacher.

above their heads and show their answers, such as, "Cards up!" or "Show me!" This way, you will be able to see all of your students' responses at the same time. If students do not raise their cards above their heads, you will not be able to see if their answers are correct, and some students may respond incompletely or may not respond at all.

Next, you will immediately provide feedback on the majority of students' responses. As seen in Figure 4.3, feedback should include a praise statement followed by the correct answer. Feedback should be delivered as quickly as possible after students respond. Make note if there is a consistent error pattern among any students, as this indicates that they are not learning the material at the same rate as the majority of the class and may need extra assistance.

Finally, *intertrial interval* is the time period between the teacher's feedback and the beginning of the next question. It is best to keep the intertrial interval short in order to maximize your rate of ASR and minimize students' opportunity to engage in off-task behaviors (Carnine, 1976; Tincani, Ernsbarger, Harrison, & Heward, 2005). An intertrial interval of 3–5 seconds should be sufficient.

> **Intertrial interval:** The time period the teacher's feedback and the next teacher-posed question.

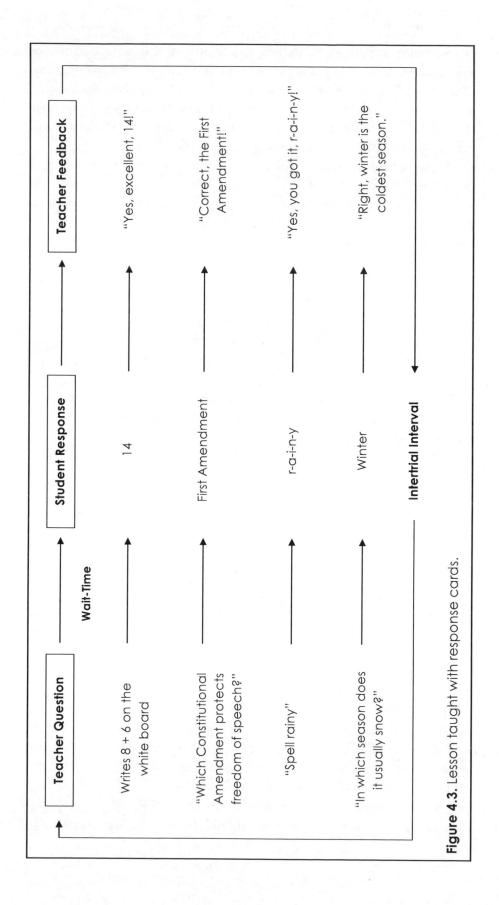

Figure 4.3. Lesson taught with response cards.

Choral Responding

Choral responding, another way to increase ASR, occurs when students vocally respond in unison to teacher-presented questions (Haydon, Mancil, & Van Loan, 2009; Heward, 1994). Like response cards, choral responding increases ASR by allowing the entire class to participate. Students who chorally respond during instruction are more engaged and less likely to perform off-task behaviors.

Teaching with choral responding involves procedures similar to those of response card lessons. The teacher presents a question to the group, allows for wait-time, and then provides a signal for students to chorally respond, followed by feedback. Choral responding can be done with the whole class or by dividing students into smaller groups. The following guidelines will help you develop lessons with choral responding (see also Heward, 1994):

- Select a series of questions that require short responses (e.g., one to three words or numbers).
- Provide a clear cue for students to respond. For example, "Tell me" or "How many" followed by a hand signal. For new or more difficult material that requires longer wait-time pauses, a cue such as "Get ready" may be helpful before you give students the cue to respond.
- Give students sufficient wait-time to formulate their answers before they respond (see Figure 4.3). One to three seconds is optimal, but new or more difficult questions may require additional wait-time.
- Provide feedback for the majority response.
- Occasionally call on individual students at random to verify correct responses.

> **Choral responding:** When students vocally respond in unison to teacher-presented questions.

Guided Notes

Guided notes are an effective approach to increase ASR for lessons involving lectures, particularly for students at the middle and high school levels. Heward (1994) defined guided notes as "teacher-prepared handouts that guide a student through a lecture with standard cues and prepared space in which to write the key facts, concepts, and/or relationships" (p. 304). Guided notes provide students with an accurate record of the lecture, and are an effective tool to improve academic per-

> **Guided notes:** Handouts for lectures that allow students to write the key facts, concepts, and/or relationships being discussed in prepared spaces.

formance (Konrad, Joseph, & Eveleigh, 2009). A sample guided notes page for a lesson on plants is found in Figure 4.4.

Guided notes are an effective classroom management and teaching tool in three important ways. First, they decrease off-task behaviors by engaging students in note-taking; students are less likely to perform off-task behaviors when they are focused on writing notes. Second, guided notes draw students' attention to salient information during the lecture. Third, because students are often poor note takers, guided notes provide a more accurate record of the lesson that can be used for study and review; this, in turn, improves performance on tests and quizzes.

Technology enables teachers to create guided notes easily. Guided notes for a lecture can be typed directly into any word processing program. Or, if you are using Microsoft PowerPoint™ to present your lectures, you can copy and paste your slides into a word processing program, and then insert spaces to create guided notes. The author of this book uses this method to create guided notes for his students.

The following guidelines will help you develop guided notes for your lectures (see also Heward, 1994):

- Provide consistent cues, such as bullet points, asterisks, and lines, so that students know where to write.
- Vary the location where students have to fill in the blank. This will maintain their attention to the guided notes and the lecture.
- Don't make students write too little or too much. The amount students write will depend on their age, academic level, and writing skills. As you deliver the lecture, periodically check to make sure students are keeping up, but not writing in their notes so quickly or so little that they can't or don't need to pay attention.
- Use follow-up activities with the guided notes, such as daily quizzes or peer tutoring activities, to ensure that students use the guided notes after they complete them.

Brisk Instructional Pacing

Brisk instructional pacing: When the teacher moves quickly through the lesson's content, minimizing down time, while giving students sufficient wait-time to answer questions.

Brisk instructional pacing means that you move quickly through the lesson's content, minimizing down time, while giving students sufficient wait-time to answer questions. Brisk instructional pacing does not mean that you hurry or rush through the lesson, but rather that you go as quickly as possible while maintaining high rates of ASR. Brisk instructional pacing increases ASR by providing more

Earth Science Guided Notes Name: ____________________

Lesson 4: Basic Parts of a Plant

- ____________________
  - » Absorb water and ____________ from the soil.
  - » Anchor the plant into the ____________.
- Leaves
  - » In the ____________, the plant uses water and air to make it grow.
  - » Leaves contain ____________, a green pigment that helps the plant make food.
- ____________________
  - » Stems hold the ____________ of the plant.
  - » Stems carry water and ____________ to all parts of the plant.
- The ____________ of the plant holds the stems.
- ____________________
  - » Attract ____________ and ____________ to the plant by their color, sweet smell, or ____________.
  - » These animals help ____________ the flower, or deliver pollen to the flower, which turns the flower into fruit.
- ____________________
  - » Contain ____________, which can grow into new plants.
  - » ____________ the seeds and holds them there until they are ____________ to get out.
- ____________________
  - » Are found inside the ____________.
  - » Carries a ____________ plant and has nutrients so the new plant can ____________.

Figure 4.4. Sample guided notes page.

Activity

Develop a lesson to teach an academic skill using one of the high ASR methods we have discussed: response cards, choral responding, or guided notes. Within your lesson plan, identify the subject matter and the students' grade level. Then, write the lesson topic, the questions you will ask, how students are expected to respond, and how you will provide feedback for correct and incorrect responses. Use the guided form below to create the lesson plan.

High Active Student Responding (ASR) Lesson Plan

Subject: _____   Grade level: _____

Type of ASR strategy (circle one):

    Response Cards   Choral Responding   Guided Notes

What is the lesson topic?

_____

_____

_____

What questions you will ask students?

_____

_____

_____

How will students be expected to respond?

_____

_____

_____

How will you provide feedback for correct and incorrect responses?

_____

_____

_____

opportunities for students to respond during the lesson (Carnine, 1976; Tincani & Crozier, 2007; Tincani et al., 2005). This decreases off-task behavior because the more students are engaged during instruction, the less opportunity they have to perform problem behaviors.

As we have seen, brisk instructional pacing can be incorporated into all of your lessons, including those with response cards and choral responding. The following considerations will help you as you develop lessons with brisk instructional pacing.

Be organized. We learned about the importance of good classroom organization to effective behavior management in Chapter 3. Being an organized teacher will also facilitate brisk instructional pacing. For instance, having individual and classwide activity schedules will produce briefer transitions, allowing more instructional time and higher rates of ASR. Just as important, making sure that all of your lesson prep is done before the lesson begins (e.g., all necessary materials are readily available to you, your teaching assistant(s), and your students), will help you teach briskly because you will not have to take time to ready instructional materials as you teach.

Minimize wait-time. As shown in Figure 4.3, wait-time is the interval between the teacher's question and the student's response. You can control the wait-time interval by presenting a cue for students to respond after you ask a question (e.g., "Tell me"). It may be helpful for you to count silently to yourself to control the duration of the wait-time interval. Generally, wait-time should be as brief as possible, 3–5 seconds or less, to promote high rates of ASR and minimize opportunities for problem behaviors. However, wait-time should be longer when (a) you are introducing new material; (b) you are asking a particularly challenging question; or (c) you are asking a question that requires a complex answer (e.g., more than one or two words) that requires thinking or collaboration among students to be answered correctly.

Minimize intertrial intervals. Intertrial interval is the time period between the teacher's feedback and the next question. You can think of intertrial intervals as the down time between learning opportunities within a lesson. Like wait-time, intertrial intervals should be brief—1–3 seconds—to increase ASR and decrease challenging behaviors. Unlike wait-time, intertrial intervals do not usually need to be longer to accommodate new, challenging, or complex material. However, if students have additional questions between learning trials, it may be necessary to extend the intertrial interval to accommodate those questions.

Provide immediate feedback. Positive or corrective feedback should be provided immediately after students respond. Ideally, positive or corrective feedback should be delivered within 1–3 seconds of students' responses.

Summary

Active student responding (ASR) occurs when a student emits a detectable response to ongoing instruction. ASR increases students' academic engagement and lessens opportunities to engage in problem behaviors. Four ways to increase ASR are response cards, choral responding, guided notes, and brisk instructional pacing. Response cards can be made inexpensively and enable students to write or select the correct answer and show their cards to the teacher. Similarly, choral responding increases ASR by allowing all students in the class to respond in unison to teacher-posed questions. Guided notes are preprinted handouts with spaces for students to write critical information about a teacher's lecture. Finally, brisk instructional pacing can be used with these and other instructional strategies to minimize down time and increase rates of ASR.

CHAPTER 5

Classroom-Wide Behavior Support

Chapter Objectives

♦ Define four basic principles of behavior that are critical in effective classroom management.

♦ Understand and implement seven classroom-wide behavior support strategies to prevent and reduce problem behaviors in your classroom.

In Chapter 1, we learned about three levels of prevention in positive behavior support: primary, secondary, and tertiary. This chapter will focus on secondary prevention or classroom-based strategies to help ensure that low-level challenging behaviors do not become persistent problems. First, we will overview four key principles of behavior—positive reinforcement, negative reinforcement, punishment, and extinction—and how they affect appropriate and challenging behaviors in the classroom. Then, we will discuss seven important classroom-wide behavior support strategies that will help you become an effective classroom manager. The strategies are (a) contingent praise and attention, (b) behavior-specific praise, (c) teaching students to recruit teacher attention, (d) error correction, (e) publicly posting classroom rules and reinforcing rule following, (f) group contingencies, and (g) active supervision.

Basic Principles of Behavior in the Classroom

What are basic principles of behavior? The word *basic* implies simple; however, in this case, basic means fundamental—principles of behavior that are common to all members of the human species, including students in your classroom. Educators focus a lot on how children are unique (and they certainly are). Even so, all children's behaviors are sensitive to four basic principles: positive reinforcement, negative reinforcement, punishment, and extinction. It is important to understand how these principles affect your students so that you can use them to promote learning and good behaviors in your classroom.

Reinforcement

Reinforcement: Any event following a behavior that increases the likelihood that the behavior will occur again.

Before we discuss the differences between positive and negative reinforcement, you should understand the general principle of *reinforcement,* which is any event following a behavior that increases the likelihood that the behavior will occur again (Cooper et al., 2007; Skinner, 1953). For example, while two of your students are quietly working, you say, "I really like the way you two are working hard," and, as a result, the students increase their time quietly working in the future.

Importantly, reinforcement is defined by its effect on behavior. If you praise a student for performing a particular behavior, but it does not increase the behavior's future occurrence, then praise is not reinforcement. A consequence is only reinforcement if it increases how much the behavior happens in the future. Therefore, what functions as reinforcement is individualized to the student, the behavior, and the situation.

Positive Reinforcement

Positive reinforcement occurs when you add something following a behavior that increases the likelihood that the behavior will occur again. Examples include praise and other forms of social recognition, tokens, money, tangible items, food, beverages, and preferred activities. From the student's perspective, positive reinforcement occurs when he performs a behavior, gets something, and consequently performs the behavior more often.

> **Positive reinforcement:** When you add something following a behavior that increases the likelihood that the behavior will occur again.

Negative Reinforcement

Negative reinforcement occurs when you remove something following a behavior that increases the likelihood that the behavior will occur again. For example, when your student politely asks if she can take a short break from a difficult assignment, you grant her request, and, as a result, she asks for breaks during difficult assignments more frequently in the future. From the student's perspective, negative reinforcement occurs when she performs a behavior, escapes or avoids something aversive, and subsequently performs the behavior more often.

> **Negative reinforcement:** When you remove something following a behavior that increases the likelihood that the behavior will occur again.

Both positive and negative reinforcement have one thing in common, they increase the future occurrence of behaviors. Negative reinforcement is sometimes confused with punishment, discussed next, which has the opposite effect on behaviors.

Activity

Identify one academic, social, or other behavior and how you would increase the behavior using *positive* reinforcement. Then, identify another academic, social, or other behavior and how you would increase the behavior using *negative* reinforcement.

- Behavior:

  _____

  _____

  _____

  _____

- Positive reinforcement:

  _____

  _____

  _____

  _____

- Behavior:

  _____

  _____

  _____

  _____

- Negative reinforcement:

  _____

  _____

  _____

  _____

Punishment

In contrast to reinforcement, *punishment* is any event following a behavior that decreases the likelihood that the behavior will occur in the future (Cooper et al., 2007; Skinner, 1953). For instance, when a student in your classroom teases another student, you say, "Stop that," and, as a result of your reprimand, the student no longer teases other students.

> **Punishment:** Any event following a behavior that decreases the likelihood that the behavior will occur in the future.

Although punishment and negative reinforcement both involve aversive stimuli as consequences, with punishment the student performs a behavior less frequently after receiving an aversive consequence. With negative reinforcement, a student performs a behavior more frequently by escaping or avoiding an aversive consequence.

As we learned in Chapter 2, the use of punishment as a classroom management technique accompanies undesirable side effects, including avoidance of environments where punishment occurs and disruptive behaviors toward the person administering punishment (Lee & Axelrod, 2005). Furthermore, although punishment can sometimes be effective in suppressing behaviors, it does not teach the student any new, appropriate behaviors to perform instead. For these reasons, punishment should be considered a technique of last resort, and should always accompany reinforcement-based techniques, including the strategies we will explore in the next section.

Extinction

Extinction, our final basic principle of behavior, is like punishment in that it results in the student performing a behavior less often. However, extinction happens when you stop delivering a reinforcer for a behavior and consequently the student performs the behavior less frequently.

> **Extinction:** When you stop delivering a reinforcer for a behavior and consequently the student performs the behavior less frequently.

The following scenario illustrates extinction. Every day you praise a student for working quietly; he stays on task as he completes his work. Therefore, praise functions as positive reinforcement. Then, you stop praising the student and subsequently he decreases the amount of time he spends on task until he is no longer completing his assignments. So by removing the reinforcer, praise, you have put the student's work behavior on extinction.

Extinction burst: When you stop delivering a reinforcer for a behavior and the frequency and/or intensity of a behavior initially increases before it decreases.

A common phenomenon often observed with extinction is *extinction burst* (Cooper et al., 2007). This happens when you stop delivering a reinforcer for a behavior and the frequency and/or intensity of a behavior initially increases before it decreases. As we will discuss in Chapter 7, extinction burst can be a problem when you are using extinction as a behavior reduction procedure because it makes withholding the reinforcer more difficult.

Classroom-Wide Behavior Support Strategies

In this section we will explore classroom-wide behavior support strategies that involve applications of the four basic principles of behavior.

Contingent Praise and Attention

Contingent praise and attention: The application of praise and other forms of attention only when the student has performed specific academic, social, or other good behaviors.

Contingent praise and attention is perhaps the most fundamental and important classroom management technique. It involves the application of praise and other forms of attention (e.g., smiles, pats on the back) only when the student has performed specific academic, social, or other good behaviors. At the same time, attention to off-task and other problem behaviors is minimized. Importantly, contingent praise and attention is most effective when delivered immediately after the target behavior occurs (Conroy, Sutherland, Snyder, & Marsh, 2008).

In their seminal study, Hall, Lund, and Jackson (1968) found that contingent praise and attention from teachers dramatically increased the study behaviors of six elementary-aged students who demonstrated low levels of study behaviors before intervention. Their simple procedure involved teachers immediately moving closer to students and providing a praise statement and gestural approval (e.g., pat on the back) when students were studying. Initially, a cue to praise students was provided to teachers by an observer; the cue was then faded.

Figure 5.1 shows the results of their study for one student, Ken. The conditions labeled baseline and reversal show Ken's percentage of studying without contingent praise and attention, and the conditions labeled reinforcement show Ken's percentage of studying with contingent praise

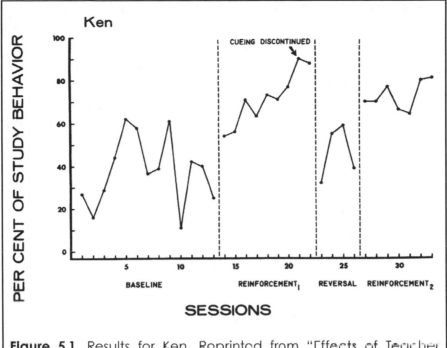

Figure 5.1. Results for Ken. Reprinted from "Effects of Teacher Attention on Study Behavior" by R. V. Hall, D. Lund, and D. Jackson, 1968, *Journal of Applied Behavior Analysis, 1*, p. 6. Copyright 1968 by the Society for the Experimental Analysis of Behavior. Reprinted with permission.

and attention. As you can see, Ken's studying behavior considerably improved when his teacher gave him praise and attention for studying.

Contingent praise and attention is an example of positive reinforcement as a classroom management technique. It is also an example of extinction; as teachers reinforce appropriate behaviors, they minimize their attention to off-task, disruptive, and other inappropriate behaviors in hope that these will decrease.

How much praise and attention should you use with your students? The question is hard to answer because, as we have discussed, reinforcement is individualized to the student, the behavior, and the situation. There are different recommendations on the best ratio of praise-to-negative interactions in the classroom. For example, Trussell (2008) recommended a 4:1 ratio of praise to negative interactions, whereas Sugai (2008) recommended an 8:1 ratio of praise to negative interactions. Regardless, it is important that you provide more praise for appropriate behaviors than you provide reprimands and other forms of negative attention for problem behaviors.

Follow these guidelines as you give students contingent praise and attention:

- Make a list of observable behaviors to reinforce with contingent praise and attention. For example, writing answers, talking quietly, taking turns, raising hands, or sharing.
- At first it will be helpful to have another person, such as a teaching assistant or coteacher, walk around the room and cue you when the students are engaging in target behaviors to reinforce them with contingent praise and attention. The cue could be as simple as pointing toward the student who needs praise and attention. You can do the same for teaching assistants and other adults working in your classroom.
- To be most effective, praise and attention should be delivered immediately after the target behavior.
- Vary the ways in which you provide contingent praise and attention. Vary your praise statements (e.g., "That's wonderful!" "You are so smart." "What a hard worker you are!") and your gestures (e.g., pats on the back, thumbs up, winks, fist bumps). Don't just say, "Good job" or repetitively issue the same praise statement.
- Minimize the attention you pay to problem behaviors. If you do, students will learn that the best way to get your attention is by being good.
- Try to maintain a ratio of at least 4:1 praise to negative statements. It may be helpful for you to count the number of times you praise students and the number of times you reprimand students during the class period to achieve this ratio.

Behavior-Specific Praise

Behavior-specific praise provides information about the type, quality, or level of a student's behaviors. We have discussed the importance of providing praise while minimizing attention to inappropriate behaviors. In addition to providing frequent and varied praise, it is beneficial to provide students with behavior-specific praise (Sutherland, Wehby, & Copeland, 2000). Behavior-specific praise gives a student important feedback on her performance and how her academic and social behaviors are improving. Like all feedback, behavior-specific praise is most effective when delivered immediately after the target behavior.

Behavior-specific praise: Praise that provides information about the type, quality, or level of a student's behaviors.

Activity

Below are examples of behavior-specific praise. The parts that are underlined indicate information about the type, quality, or level of a student's behaviors. See if you can provide three behavior-specific praise examples of your own:

- "Joel, I really liked the way you <u>raised your hand and waited patiently</u>."

- "Lupé, that was a great job <u>writing your name neatly</u>."

- "You <u>got all of your math problems correct</u>, Amy, excellent!"

- "Rashad, <u>very nice sharing with your partner</u>."

- _____

  _____

  _____

  _____

- _____

  _____

  _____

  _____

- _____

  _____

  _____

  _____

- _____

  _____

  _____

  _____

Teaching Students to Recruit Teacher Attention

You have learned about the importance of teacher praise and attention; however, many students are not proficient at getting the teacher's attention when they need help with an assignment or they have done something that deserves recognition. Consequently, students may miss critical opportunities for teacher attention, including praise.

> **Teaching students to recruit teacher attention:** Instructions, prompts, and reinforcement to help students to independently get the teacher's attention when they have completed their work or need help from the teacher to complete their work.

Teaching students to recruit teacher attention involves instructions, prompts, and reinforcement to help students to independently get the teacher's attention when they have completed their work or need help from the teacher to complete their work (Alber & Heward, 1997). Teaching students to recruit teacher attention has been shown to increase the frequency of teacher praise statements, as well as the amount of work items and the accuracy of work items completed by students (Alber, Heward, & Hippler, 1999; Craft, Alber, & Heward, 1998).

Your students could benefit from learning to recruit teacher attention if (a) they do not independently raise their hands when they have a question or need help with assignments, or (b) they do not independently get your attention for feedback when they have completed a portion or all of their assignments. Craft and colleagues (1998) described the following steps to teach students to recruit teacher attention.

Explain to students why it is important to recruit teacher attention. Reasons include that it helps students get their work done, improves their grades, and makes them feel good when they receive praise for doing their work completely and correctly.

Explain when and how often it is appropriate to ask for attention. You can use a think-aloud technique to illustrate when it is appropriate for students to seek attention (e.g., "I'm finished with half of my problems, let's see how the teacher thinks I'm doing. Is she busy with other students? No. I'll raise my hand"). You can also provide specific instructions for when to seek attention, such as when the student's work is about halfway finished, when the student's work is totally finished, when the student doesn't understand instructions, or when the student is uncertain if he has answered a question or problem correctly. It is a good idea to instruct the student to look and see if the teacher is not busy before he raises his hand.

Model and describe appropriate ways to get teacher attention. Students can be taught to raise their hands and wait to be recognized by the teacher, or to approach the teacher while she is at her desk (and not busy) to seek feedback. Phrases such as "Is this right?" or "How am

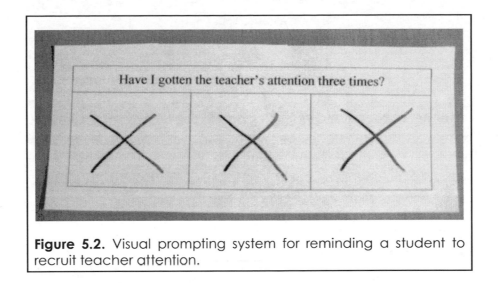

Figure 5.2. Visual prompting system for reminding a student to recruit teacher attention.

I doing?" or "I don't understand this" can be modeled to demonstrate appropriate ways to solicit attention. Finally, you should give students a target for the number of times to recruit your attention during a class period such as three times during English class.

Provide prompts for recruiting teacher attention. Prior to the beginning of class, you should provide a reminder to students about how, when, and how many times to seek the teacher's attention. A visual prompting system, such as you see in Figure 5.2, may be helpful in reminding students to recruit teacher attention. Each time the student recruits attention, he puts a check in the box. When all three boxes are checked, he knows that he has met his goal for the class period.

Positively reinforce recruiting teacher attention. At the end of the class period, review and provide behavior-specific feedback to the student on how he recruits teacher attention. If the student has met a specific goal (e.g., three times during one class period), you might provide a reward.

Error Correction

Your students will sometimes make mistakes while performing academic or social skills. It is important that you do not simply let mistakes go; if you do, your students will practice errors and will have more difficulty mastering skills. *Error correction* occurs when a teacher systematically responds to an error to increase the student's accuracy with a skill. Error correction alone or in combination with other strategies has been shown to increase students' accuracy with spelling (Barbetta, Heron, & Heward, 1993; Grskovic

> **Error correction:** When a teacher systematically responds to an error to increase the student's accuracy with a skill.

Activity

Identify a student you teach who is poor at recruiting teacher attention, or think of a hypothetical student you might teach who is poor at recruiting teacher attention. Describe how you will teach the student to recruit teacher attention by explaining why it is important, when and how often to recruit teacher attention, and how to get the teacher's attention. Also, describe how you will prompt and reinforce the student for appropriately getting the teacher's attention.

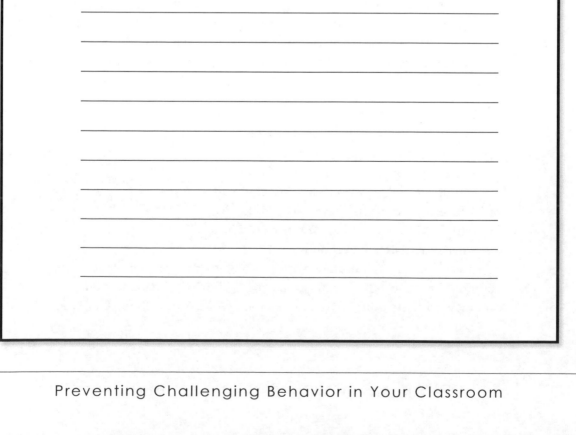

& Belfiore, 1996), geography facts (Barbetta & Heward, 1993), math (Maheady, Sacca, & Harper, 1987), purchasing retail items (Xin, Grasso, Dipipi-Hoy, & Jitendra, 2005), and social skills (Lalli, Pinter-Lalli, Mace, & Murphy, 1991).

Successful error correction strategies share these key components, which comprise an error correction sequence:

- *Immediate.* The teacher performs error correction immediately after the student has made an error.
- *Modeling.* The teacher models the correct response by saying it, writing it, or showing the student how to perform the skill correctly.
- *Active responding.* The teacher has the student perform the correct response following the model.
- *Independent practice.* The teacher gives the student an independent opportunity to perform the skill without the teacher's prompt. Typically, the teacher will require different responses before returning to the skill.

Figure 5.3 illustrates two error correction sequences for geography facts and spelling.

Posting Classroom Rules and Reinforcing Rule Following

Publicly posting classroom rules and reinforcing rule following is another critical strategy to promote good behaviors in your classroom (Conroy et al., 2008; Greenwood, Hops, Delquadri, & Guild, 1974; Johnson, Stoner, & Green, 1996). Publicly posted rules clearly communicate your expectations to students and are most effective when combined with positive reinforcement, including behavior-specific praise, for following the rules (Greenwood et al., 1974). These guidelines will help you develop effective rules for your classroom:

- Make three to five positively stated rules. Positively stated means that the rules identify what students are supposed to do (e.g., "Be respectful to your classmates") as opposed to what students are not supposed to do (e.g., "Don't be disrespectful to your classmates"). Avoid writing negatively stated rules because they do not tell the student what to do and they encourage the use of punishment when rules are not followed.
- If possible, involve your students in the creation of classroom rules. This will encourage buy-in and will increase the likelihood that students follow the rules.

Teacher: "What is the capitol of Washington?"		Teacher: "Spell 'fighter'."
Student: "Seattle."		Student: 'f-i-t-e-r'
Teacher (modeling correct response): "No. Tacoma."		(Teacher models correct response by telling student to erase the first "t" and add "gh.")
Student (actively responds to teacher model): "Tacoma."		Student (actively responds to teacher model): "f-i-g-h-t-e-r"
Teacher: "Yes. Tacoma."		Teacher: "Good, 'fighter.'"
(Teacher asks a few different questions.)		(Teacher has the student spell several different words.)
Teacher (provides opportunity for independent practice): "What is the capitol of Washington?"		Teacher (provides opportunity for independent practice): "Spell 'fighter.'"
Student: "Tacoma."		Student: "f-i-g-h-t-e-r"
Teacher: "Correct, Tacoma."		Teacher: "That's right. 'Fighter.'"

Figure 5.3. Two error correction sequences for geography facts and spelling.

Rules	Behavior-Specific Expectations
Respect your classmates.	Use polite words when you talk to other students. Share when you have extra of something. Be quiet when other students are working. Say hello to other students as they enter the classroom. Only touch other students in a friendly way (e.g., handshake, high five).
Always try your hardest.	Keep working until you have answered all of the questions. Double check your work before you turn it in. If you are not sure about a problem, try your best to answer. If you feel frustrated, raise your hand to ask the teacher a question. If you finish early, find another activity to do.
Listen to the teacher.	Wait for the teacher to call on you before you talk. Listen carefully to the teacher's instructions before you begin. Ask the teacher before you leave the classroom. If you are unsure if it is OK to do something, ask the teacher first. When the teacher says, "Finished," put your work away and get ready for the next activity.

Figure 5.4. Examples of classroom rules and behavior-specific expectations.

- Post your rules in a prominent location in the classroom (e.g., on the front board). Make the rules large enough that your students can see them from anywhere in your classroom.
- Spend at least 5–10 minutes teaching each of the rules, including examples and nonexamples of rule following. This could be done at the beginning of the school year. Examples of classroom rules and behavior-specific expectations are shown in Figure 5.4. You could also have students role-play following the rules.
- Provide behavior-specific feedback and praise to students for following the rules. For instance, if one of your classroom rules is "Listen to the teacher," then an example of behavior-specific praise would be "Josh, I like the way you finished your worksheet when I asked you—that's a great example of listening to the teacher."
- Provide a reinforcer from your group-contingency system, discussed next, for students who follow the rules.

Group Contingencies

Group contingencies are another effective way to prevent and reduce problem behaviors in the classroom (Stage & Quiroz, 1997). Group contingencies are special reinforcement systems in which part or all of the

Activity

Write a set of three to five positively stated rules for your classroom or a hypothetical classroom. Describe where you will post the rules, how you will teach the rules, and how you will recognize students for following the rules.

_____

_____

_____

_____

_____

_____

_____

_____

_____

_____

_____

_____

_____

_____

_____

_____

_____

_____

class must perform appropriate behaviors to earn a reward (Hulac & Benson, 2010). There are a number of ways to implement group contingencies in the classroom (Skinner, Williams, & Neddenriep, 2004); however, we will focus on two strategies: *independent group contingencies*, including classroom-wide token systems, and *dependent group contingencies*, such as the good behavior game.

Independent group contingencies involve each student earning rewards for her own behaviors. *Classroom-wide token systems* are a type of independent group contingency in which the teacher makes the delivery of a reward contingent on each student earning a specified number of tokens, which are then exchanged for a back-up reward. Classroom-wide token systems have important advantages as a reinforcement technique. First, they enable the teacher to arrange powerful rewards to reinforce students' appropriate behaviors. This is especially important because teacher praise and attention may not always be reinforcing for students' behaviors. Second, they enable the teacher to reinforce many different behaviors with tokens, and students learn that they must work over an extended period of time to earn the back-up reward.

These guidelines will help you implement a classroom-wide token system:

- Select a group of reasonable rewards for students to earn with tokens. Rewards earned on a daily basis could include stickers, pencils, small edible items (e.g., mini candy bars), or brief activities (e.g., an extra 5 minutes on the computer). Larger rewards earned on a weekly basis could include lunch with the teacher, a trip into the community, being class helper for a day, or a free pass to hand in instead of homework.

- It is preferable to offer a limited selection of rewards, and to have students chose which reward they will earn.

- When you introduce a classroom-wide token system, it is better to have students work for smaller rewards on a daily basis, rather than larger rewards on a weekly basis. For example, you could have students select a small reward to earn at the end of the class period if they have accumulated a small number of tokens (e.g., five). You can then progressively thin the schedule of reinforce-

> **Dependent group contingencies:** A type of group contingency in which students earn rewards as a group contingent upon some or all of the group's behavior.
>
> **Group contingencies:** Special reinforcement systems in which part or all of the class must perform appropriate behaviors to earn a reward.
>
> **Independent group contingencies:** A type of group contingency in which each student earns rewards for her own behaviors.
>
> **Classroom-wide token systems:** A type of independent group contingency in which the teacher makes the delivery of a reward contingent on each student earning a specified number of tokens, which are then exchanged for a back-up reward.

ment to have students earn more tokens over longer periods or work for larger rewards.

- Select your tokens. Tokens can be made from a variety of items such as pennies or erasers. Tokens can also be tally marks on a piece of paper or stars drawn with a dry erase marker on laminated paper.
- Tokens can be placed on a token board, which can have a space for the student to write what she is earning (see Figure 5.5). This will serve as a reminder for the student about the contingency in effect.
- Select the amount of tokens the student will earn for the reward. The number of tokens earned should correspond to the magnitude of the reward (e.g., sticker = 5 tokens; 5 minutes extra time at recess = 25 tokens; lunch with teacher = 75 tokens).
- Immediately deliver tokens for appropriate behaviors, including those specified by your classroom rules. Occasionally accompany the delivery of tokens with behavior-specific praise.
- When students have earned the requisite number of tokens, have them "cash in" by handing you their tokens or by counting the number of tally marks they have accumulated in exchange for the back-up reward.

Good behavior game: A type of dependent group contingency in which the class is divided into two teams that compete for a reward based upon which team displays the fewest problem behaviors.

Dependent group contingencies involve students earning rewards as a group contingent upon some or all of the group's behavior. The *good behavior game* is a dependent group contingency in which the class is divided into two teams that compete for a reward based upon which team displays the fewest problem behaviors (Barrish, Saunders, & Wolf, 1969; Dolan, Kellam, Brown, & Werthamer-Larsson, 1993; Harris & Sherman, 1973). To play the good behavior game with students in your classroom, you can:

- Identify a set of inappropriate behaviors that students should not perform in your classroom during the period (e.g., talking-out, aggression, cursing, stealing from other students).
- Divide the classroom into two groups.
- Identify a reward for the winning team.
- Explain to students that they will be competing against each other for which team has the fewest problem behaviors and that the team with the fewest problem behaviors will earn a reward. Describe each of the targeted problem behaviors to the class.

Figure 5.5. Sample token board.

- Make a tally mark on the board every time a member of each team engages in one of the challenging behaviors. You will have two sets of tally marks on the board, one for each team.
- The team with the fewest tally marks at the end of the period will earn the reward. If both teams have a low number of tally marks (e.g., less than five), then both teams can earn the reward.

Randomization is one way to increase the effectiveness of both independent and dependent group contingency systems (Hulac & Benson, 2010). Randomization makes group contingency systems more motivating by having students guess about the contingency. To randomize your group contingency system, you could (a) have students work for a secret reward contained in a "surprise" box; (b) once students have earned the back-up reward, spin a wheel and have students earn whatever reward the wheel points to; or (c) in a dependent group contingency system, select a small group of students in the class at random (e.g., by picking names out of a hat) and make the entire class's reward contingent on their behaviors. For example, if members of the randomly selected group complete their homework then the entire class will earn a reward.

Active Supervision

Active supervision means the teacher actively looks around the classroom, moves around the classroom, and interacts with students to prevent instances of problem behaviors (Colvin, Sugai, Good, & Lee, 1997; De Pry & Sugai, 2002; Johnson-Gros, Lyons, & Griffin, 2008). Active supervision is important because it enables the teacher to catch students being good and to provide reminders about appropriate behaviors. When implementing active supervision, it is essential to give students behavior-specific praise for rule following and to provide tokens or rewards from your group-contingency system when students engage in good behaviors.

> **Active supervision:** When the teacher actively looks around the classroom, moves around the classroom, and interacts with students to prevent instances of problem behaviors.

Precorrections are an important component of active supervision. Precorrections are reminders for students to engage in appropriate behaviors and to refrain from inappropriate behaviors. Importantly, precorrections are given to students before challenging behaviors occur and not after. Precorrections can be given to individual students or the whole class at the beginning of the period, or they can be given periodically throughout the period. Examples of precorrections include:

> **Precorrections:** Reminders for students to engage in appropriate behaviors and to refrain from inappropriate behaviors.

- "Remember, when you have a question, raise your hand and wait to be called on."
- "'Listen to the teacher' is a classroom rule, so listen for my instructions before you begin."
- "We use polite words in this class, so please refrain from saying mean words when you speak to your classmates."

Summary

Four basic principles of behavior that are critical in classroom management are positive reinforcement, negative reinforcement, punishment, and extinction. Positive reinforcement occurs when you add something following a behavior that increases the likelihood that the behavior will occur again; negative reinforcement occurs when you remove something following a behavior that increases the likelihood that the behavior will occur again. Punishment is any event following a behavior that decreases the likelihood that the behavior will occur in the future. Finally, extinction happens when you stop delivering a reinforcer for a behavior and, consequently, the student performs the behavior less frequently.

The chapter described seven classroom-wide strategies for preventing challenging behaviors. Contingent praise and attention is the application of praise and attention only when the student has performed specific academic, social, or other good behaviors. Behavior-specific praise is a type of contingent praise in which the student receives specific feedback on her performance and how her academic and social behaviors are improving. All praise should be given immediately after appropriate behaviors occur. Teaching students to recruit teacher attention involves instructions, prompts, and reinforcement to help students independently get the teacher's attention when they have completed their work or need help from the teacher to complete their work. Error correction is when a teacher systematically responds to an error to increase the student's accuracy with a skill.

Publicly posting classroom rules and reinforcing rule following is an excellent way to communicate your behavioral expectations to students. Group contingencies are special reinforcement systems in which part or all of the class must perform appropriate behaviors to earn a reward. Classroom-wide token systems are a type of group contingency in which the teacher makes the delivery of a reward contingent on each student earning a specified number of tokens, while the good behavior game involves dividing the class into two teams that compete for a reward based upon which team displays the fewest problem behaviors. Finally, active supervision means the teacher actively looks around the classroom, moves around the classroom, and interacts with students to prevent instances of problem behaviors. Precorrections are an essential part of active supervision in which students given are reminders to engage in appropriate behaviors and to refrain from inappropriate behaviors.

CHAPTER 6

Functional Behavioral Assessment

Chapter Objectives

♦ Define functional behavioral assessment (FBA) and describe why educators should conduct FBA.

♦ Identify the environmental reasons why students engage in challenging behaviors.

♦ Understand the three steps for conducting FBA.

♦ Describe how the process of FBA informs behavior intervention programming.

Some of your students will require individualized, function-based interventions to reduce their chronic challenging behaviors. In this chapter, you will learn how to conduct functional behavioral assessment to identify why students engage in difficult behaviors. We will explore the variables that lead to challenging behaviors, namely, motivating operations, antecedents, and consequences. We will then discuss methods for conducting functional behavioral assessment, including indirect assessment, direct assessment, and functional analysis.

What Is Functional Behavioral Assessment and Why Do We Do It?

Functional behavioral assessment (FBA): A collection of strategies to identify the environmental reasons why students engage in challenging behaviors for the purpose of developing effective interventions. These include indirect assessments, direct assessments, and functional analysis.

Functional behavioral assessment (FBA) is a collection of strategies to identify the environmental reasons why students engage in challenging behaviors for the purpose of developing effective interventions (Alberto & Troutman, 2009; Cooper et al., 2007; Heron & Harris, 2001). The environmental reasons for challenging behaviors are often found in the classroom. For example, a student engages in problem behaviors to escape or avoid a classroom activity that he finds aversive. In Chapter 2, we discussed alterable variables, which are things the teacher can control to change student learning and behavior (Bloom, 1980; Heward, 2003). FBA guides us toward manipulating the right alterable variables to prevent and reduce problem behaviors in the classroom.

Therefore, if the student's FBA tells us that he engages in problem behaviors to escape or avoid an aversive activity, we could offer him a choice of activities, or we could teach him a more appropriate way to escape, such as by asking for a break or by requesting to do an alternate activity. We will discuss function-based intervention strategies in Chapter 7.

FBA is an essential part of developing a behavior intervention plan (BIP), a written plan that describes procedures to prevent and reduce a student's challenging behaviors. Children with disabilities who engage in challenging behaviors that interfere with their learning should receive individualized interventions based in positive behavior support. Specifically, when developing a student's Individualized Education Program (IEP), the team must:

In the case of a child whose behavior impedes the child's learning or that of others, consider the use of *positive behavioral interventions and supports*, and other strategies, to address that behavior (Individuals with Disabilities Education Improvement Act of 2004, H.R. 1350, Sec. 300.324(a)(2)(i); emphasis added).

BIPs that are informed by data collected from an FBA are more likely to be successful than BIPs that are not (Carter & Horner, 2007, 2009). For instance, if a student engages in destructive behaviors to escape from aversive classroom activities, we could use classroom rules, behavior-specific praise, and a group contingency system to teach appropriate behaviors (see Chapter 5); however, even with these interventions, the student will likely continue to be disruptive until we implement strategies to address the behavior's functions. Specifically, we could make classroom activities less aversive, or we could teach her more appropriate ways to seek escape. If disruption is reinforced by teacher attention, we could teach her more appropriate ways to seek teacher attention or provide her with more attention on a noncontingent basis.

Why Do Students Engage in Challenging Behaviors?

Challenging behaviors can seem like they come from nowhere; however, there are almost always specific environmental reasons why students engage in these behaviors. Next, we will explore the three environmental variables that maintain most difficult behaviors. The environmental variables are motivating operations, triggering antecedents, and reinforcing consequences.

Motivating Operations

Motivating operations (MOs) alter the momentary value of reinforcers and the frequency of behaviors associated with those reinforcers (Laraway, Snycerski, Michael, & Poling, 2003). For example, if a child is deprived of food for a period of time (MO), then food will become momentarily more reinforcing, and behaviors associated with producing food (e.g., asking for a snack) will increase in frequency. In a different example, if a child becomes sick from

> **Motivating operations (MOs):** Events that alter the momentary value of reinforcers and the frequency of behaviors associated with those reinforcers.

a virus (MO), then escape-maintained behaviors may be momentarily more reinforcing. If she is presented with an assignment she doesn't like, she may, pinch, hit, or engage in other disruptive behaviors that result in escape from the assignment.

Importantly, MOs are often temporally distant from the behaviors they affect (Ray & Watson, 2001). This means that a relevant MO could happen hours before the student engages in challenging behaviors. For instance, a child's sleep deprivation the night before may serve as an MO for difficult behaviors throughout the school day. The temporally distant nature of MOs presents a challenge to accurately identifying them in an FBA. Often, it is necessary to communicate with parents and staff in other settings to determine the presence of temporally distant MOs.

Common examples of MOs that affect challenging behaviors are:
- difficulty with the morning routine (e.g., getting up late, missing the bus);
- argument before school;
- argument in another class;
- medication change;
- illness;
- sleep deprivation;
- change in family members present in the home setting;
- traumatic event at home;
- lack of attention from staff or peers;
- presence or absence of a specific staff person;
- presence or absence of a specific classmate;
- unpredictable schedule;
- loss of a preferred activity; and
- disorganized transitions.

Antecedents

Antecedents are stimuli that trigger challenging behaviors. Often, antecedents involve the presentation of difficult tasks, unclear instructions, or the presence of nonpreferred people. In the presence of these stimuli, the student may engage in disruptive behaviors to escape from or avoid them. For instance, when the teacher gives the student a hard assignment, he hits another student, and then he is sent out of the classroom (and thus the demand is terminated). Antecedents also involve the presentation of preferred stimuli, such as preferred food and drink, preferred activities, and preferred people. In the presence of these

Antecedents: Stimuli that trigger challenging behaviors.

stimuli, the student will engage in challenging behaviors to obtain them. For example, a teacher places a container of juice on the table and the student screams so that she will pour him a cup.

Reinforcing Consequences

As we learned in Chapter 5, reinforcement is any event following a behavior that increases the likelihood that the behavior will occur again. Positive reinforcement happens when you add something following a behavior that increases the likelihood that the behavior will occur again. For instance, one student pinches another student to get a toy, she takes the toy, and, consequently, she pinches more often in the future. Negative reinforcement happens when you remove something following a behavior that increases the likelihood that the behavior will occur again. For example, a student screams when the teacher presents a demand, the teacher removes the demand, and consequently the student screams more frequently to escape or avoid demands in the future.

The diagrams in Figure 6.1 show how MOs, antecedents, positive reinforcement, and negative reinforcement control challenging behaviors. The first two examples depict behaviors maintained by negative reinforcement; the next two examples depict behaviors maintained by positive reinforcement.

It is important to note that well-intentioned consequences can actually strengthen problem behaviors. For example, the second diagram in Figure 6.1 shows the teacher giving the student a break after the student hits and screams in the presence of a difficult assignment. Presumably, the teacher wants to let the student "cool down" until he is ready for the assignment; however, the teacher is inadvertently reinforcing these problem behaviors by allowing the student to escape. It is therefore critical to understand the functions of problem behaviors before you develop interventions.

Conducting FBA

Step 1: Define the Problem Behaviors

The first step in conducting an FBA is to define the problem behaviors. One way to accomplish this is to talk with people who spend time with the student—teaching assistants, other school staff, and parents— and ask them to tell you what the problem behavior looks like and where it is most likely to occur. You can observe the student in the classroom

Activity

Below are two sets of boxes. Beneath the boxes, identify hypothetical MOs, antecedents, and consequences maintaining two different problem behaviors.

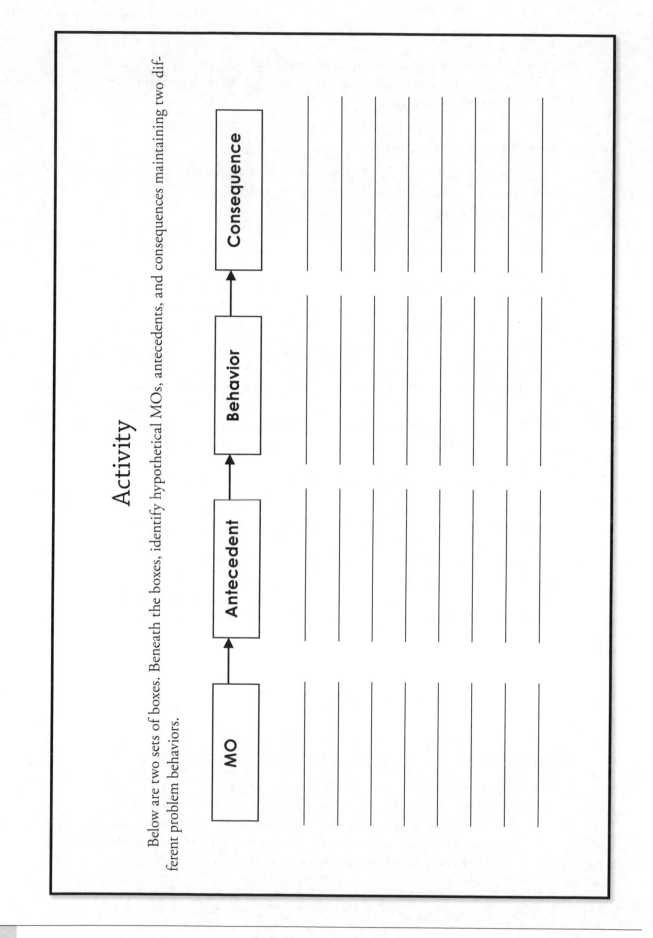

| MO | Antecedent | Behavior | Consequence |

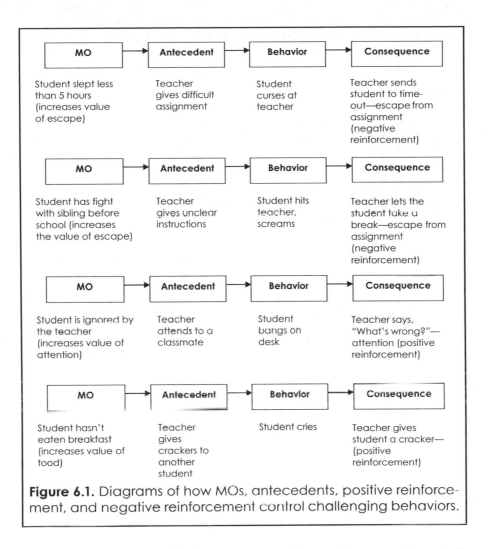

Figure 6.1. Diagrams of how MOs, antecedents, positive reinforcement, and negative reinforcement control challenging behaviors.

or other settings to verify the presence and form of target responses. It will be helpful for you to ask if there are any specific routines (e.g., times or day, class periods, activities) in which problem behaviors are more likely. This will give you a clear picture of the behaviors and will focus your assessment efforts on the daily routines where difficulties are most likely. Some FBA questionnaires and rating scales, discussed in the next section, include specific questions about challenging behavior definitions and problematic daily routines.

It is critical to define problem behaviors in objective and observable terms (Scott, Anderson, & Spaulding, 2008). This means that you define each behavior in a clear and precise way so that you and others can measure it. Examples of behaviors that are not defined in objective and measurable terms include "disruption," "frustration," "anger," and "disrespect." Objective and observable definitions of these behaviors could be "hitting and screaming," "tearing work materials," "pounding the desk," and "cursing." The more specifically you write your definitions, the better.

Step 2: Gather Information

Once you have defined the problem behaviors, the next step is to gather information to form hypotheses about environmental variables that support the behaviors. There are many different methods to gather information for the FBA. These can be classified into three types: indirect assessment, direct assessment, and functional analysis (Heron & Harris, 2001). We will explore the procedures, advantages, and disadvantages associated with each.

Indirect assessment. *Indirect assessment* involves interviewing people who know the student to gather information about variables maintaining problem behaviors. Indirect assessment can be done informally by asking questions about potential behavior functions. It is not recommended that you rely exclusively on informal interview data for the FBA because what you learn is likely to be subjective or biased or may omit important information about the target responses and their functions.

Formal indirect assessments include questionnaires and rating scales to systematically identify behavior functions. Formal indirect assessments have three advantages as information-gathering tools. First, they provide structure to the process and guide the interviewer through questions that seek to identify a number of maintaining variables. Second, they allow the interviewer to gather information from multiple individuals. Finally, they are relatively easy and convenient to implement, particularly those assessments that involve rating scales that can be completed independently in a short period of time.

> **Formal indirect assessments:** Questionnaires and rating scales to systematically identify behavior functions.
>
> **Indirect assessment:** Interviewing people who know the student to gather information about variables maintaining problem behaviors.

Table 6.1 shows five formal indirect assessment tools. The first two instruments, the Functional Assessment Checklist: Teachers and Staff (FACTS; March et al., 2000) and the Functional Assessment Interview form (FAI; O'Neill et al., 1997) are semi-structured interviews that seek to identify setting events (MOs), antecedents, reinforcing consequences, and other variables relevant to problem behaviors (e.g., student's medical history, previous interventions, communication skills). Semi-structured interviews provide comprehensive information that enables the evaluator to form hypothesis statements about variables related to problem responses. However, semi-structured interviews may take some time to complete, particularly if they contain a large number of items (e.g., FAI) and are administered to several persons.

Table 6.1

Examples of Formal Indirect Assessment Tools

Instrument	Authors / Date	Type of Assessment	Procedures
Functional Assessment Checklist: Teachers and Staff (FACTS)	March et al. (2000)	Semi-structured interview	Two-part interview to identify problem behaviors, routines in which problem behaviors are most likely, and maintaining variables, including setting events (MOs), antecedents, and consequences. Concludes with a summary of problem behavior functions. Administered to teachers, staff, parents, or others who know the student.
Functional Assessment Interview	O'Neill et al. (1997)	Semi-structured interview	Interview with 11 sections of questions to identify setting events (MOs), antecedents, consequences, communication skills, and previous interventions. Designed to be used with the Functional Assessment Observation form.
Functional Analysis Screening Tool (FAST)	Iwata & DeLeon (2005)	Semi-structured interview and rating scale	Includes 16 yes/no questions to identify consequences maintaining problem behaviors. Intended as a screening tool to guide functional analysis.
Motivation Assessment Scale (MAS)	Durand & Crimmins (1988)	Rating scale	Contains 16 Likert scale questions to identify consequences maintaining problem behaviors.
Questions About Behavioral Function (QABF)	Matson & Vollmer (1995)	Rating scale	Uses 25 Likert-scale questions to determine consequences maintaining problem behaviors.

In contrast, the next three assessments in Table 6.1, the Functional Analysis Screening Tool (FAST; Iwata & DeLeon, 2005), Motivation Assessment Scale (MAS; Durand & Crimmins, 1988), and Questions About Behavioral Function (QABF; Matson & Vollmer, 1995), are rating scales in which the interviewee rates the likelihood of problem behaviors occurring in the presence of various consequences. Ranging from

16 to 25 items, these instruments require less time to complete than semi-structured interviews. However, rating scales yield limited information about behavior functions; most identify consequences reinforcing problem behaviors, but do not yield information about problem routines, MOs, or triggering antecedents.

Indirect assessment provides convenient information about behavior functions; however, indirect assessment is inherently subjective because it evaluates team members' perceptions of why problem behaviors occur, which may or may not reflect actual maintaining variables. A more accurate approach is to combine indirect assessment with direct assessment.

Direct assessment. *Direct assessment* means observing the student in settings where problem behaviors occur and collecting data to discover patterns between antecedents, behaviors, and consequences. Direct assessment is potentially more accurate than indirect assessment because it involves direct confirmation of patterns between behaviors and environmental events. Direct assessment is usually more effortful and time consuming than indirect assessment, although it yields more reliable information.

> **Direct assessment:** Observing the student in settings where problem behaviors occur and collecting data to discover patterns between antecedents, behaviors, and consequences.

There are myriad ways to perform direct assessment, including scatter plots (Touchette, MacDonald, & Langer, 1985), ABC assessment (Bijou, Peterson, & Ault, 1968), and the Functional Assessment Observation form (O'Neill et al., 1997). Scatter plots involve creating a grid to identify patterns in problem behaviors across time. The vertical axis of the grid segments time into hours, half hours, quarter hours, or any time unit appropriate to the student's schedule. The horizontal access segments the grid into successive days. Each box on the grid is shaded when the problem behavior occurs during the interval or left unshaded when the problem behavior does not occur during the interval. Partial shading indicates that the behavior happened one to four times, while full shading indicates that the behavior happened five or more times. At the end of the week, the scatter plot can be visually inspected to determine if there are consistent patterns between times or day and occurrence of problem responses. Scatter plots do not identify specific antecedents and consequences; however, they lead the assessor to events that reliably coincide with problem behavior episodes.

Figure 6.2 shows a hypothetical scatter plot with data. The shaded areas indicate intervals in which hitting occurred. The data suggest that hitting most often happened between 2 p.m. and 3 p.m. Thus, we can conclude that whatever activities were happening between 2 p.m. and 3 p.m. are related to hitting. Therefore, our interventions should focus on

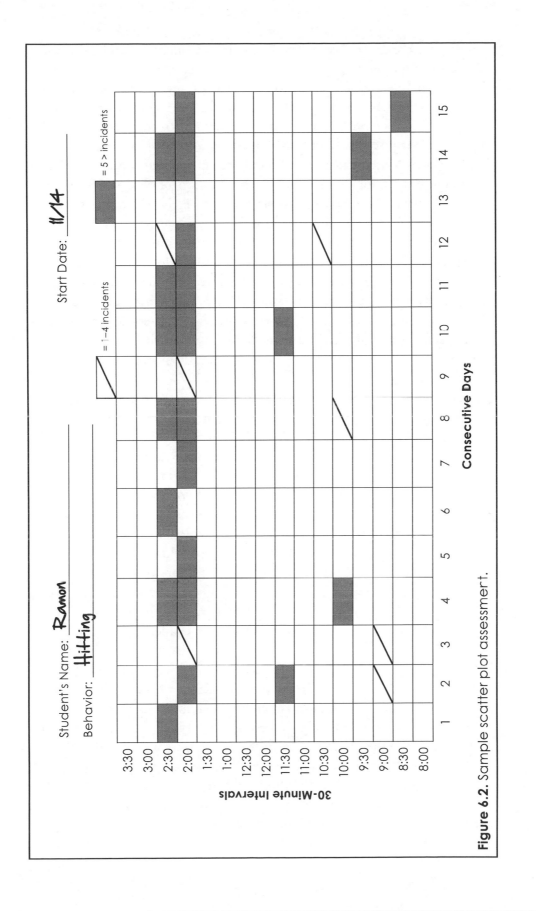

Figure 6.2. Sample scatter plot assessment.

modifying these activities so that they are less likely to evoke the student's hitting response.

In ABC assessment, the observer records every instance of the challenging behavior, including the time the behavior occurred, what happened just before the behavior, and what happened just after the behavior. The purpose of ABC assessment is to establish patterns of antecedents and consequences over time to determine behavioral functions (see Figure 6.3). For example, if after several days of observation transitions consistently precede aggression, then it is likely that these are antecedents for aggression. Similarly, if being redirected by the teacher is a reliable consequence to aggression, the redirection is probably reinforcing aggression. Understanding the antecedents and reinforcing consequences for problem behaviors allows us to develop interventions to modify them.

Finally, the Functional Assessment Observation form is a structured direct assessment tool that combines elements of scatter plot assessment and ABC assessment. The Functional Assessment Observation form is intended to be used with the Functional Assessment Interview form to confirm behavioral functions (O'Neill et al., 1997). The observer collects data on antecedents and consequences for challenging behaviors within a grid, which enables the observer to establish patterns between times of day, antecedents, consequences, and problem behaviors.

Functional analysis. *Functional analysis* is the experimental manipulation of variables thought to maintain challenging behaviors (Iwata, Dorsey, Slifer, Bauman, & Richman, 1982/1994). Unlike direct assessment, the professional conducting functional analysis sets up conditions—or experimental analogs—in which the problem behavior is likely to occur. For example, if the professional thinks the behavior is maintained by escape from task demands, the experimenter will give the student a demanding task and will remove the task when the student performs the challenging behavior. If the behavior occurs under these circumstances, then it is probably maintained by escape from task demands. Typically, the professional alternates different conditions, including escape, attention, tangible reinforcement, or play (control condition), to see if a differentially higher rate of behavior occurs in one or more conditions. There are different formats to conduct functional analysis, including extended and brief analyses (Tincani, Castrogiavanni, & Axelrod, 1999) and classroom-based assessments (Ellis & Magee, 1999). Functional analysis is the most resource intensive and time consuming of the FBA methods we have discussed and should only be conducted by highly

Functional analysis: Experimental manipulation of variables thought to maintain challenging behaviors for the purpose of identifying behavior functions.

Student: Lisa		Observer: Ms. Ramirez	Date: 9/17
Time begin: 8:00		Time end: 3:00	

Time	Antecedent	Behavior	Consequence
8:56 a.m.	Transition	Pinching	Redirected by teacher
9:29 a.m.	Transition	Hitting	Redirected by teacher
10:48 a.m.	Worksheet	Tearing	Time-out

Figure 6.3. Sample ABC assessment.

trained professionals. Thus, functional analysis is typically not the assessment methodology of choice to complete an FBA in school settings.

Step 3: Form Hypothesis Statements

After you gather information, the final step of the FBA is to form hypotheses about the variables maintaining each challenging behavior. A hypothesis is simply an educated guess about the environmental reasons for each behavior based on the assessment data you gathered in Step 2. Hypotheses can be stated in a narrative format or, as shown in Figures 6.1 and 6.4, can be diagrammed according to the MOs, antecedents, and reinforcing consequences for each problem response.

Because MOs are often temporally distant from problem behaviors, you may not be able to pinpoint the MO for a particular response. This is reflected in the spaces with question marks under the MO variable in Figure 6.4. It is also important to note that some problem behaviors may have multiple MOs, antecedents, or maintaining consequences. In these cases, it is best to diagram each set of contingencies separately, as you see in the first two diagrams of Figure 6.4. In this example, it appears that yelling and cursing are maintained by both positive reinforcement in the form of attention and negative reinforcement in the form of escape. Therefore, any behavior intervention strategy should address both of these maintaining consequences.

Critically, the FBA and resulting hypothesis statements are not the final product of the process. The final product is a successful intervention plan that reduces the student's challenging behaviors. If the resulting behavior interventions are not successful, the team may need to reflect on the data gathered in the FBA and reconsider its hypotheses statements or, if necessary, collect additional data to pinpoint controlling variables. In

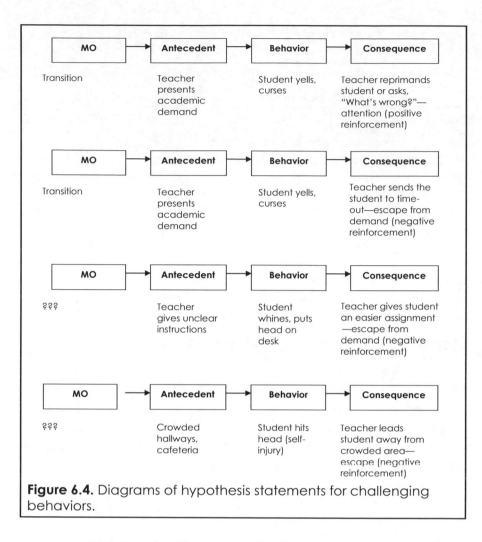

Figure 6.4. Diagrams of hypothesis statements for challenging behaviors.

essence, an FBA is useless if it does not lead to a reduction in the student's challenging behaviors.

Putting It Together: FBA and Behavior Intervention Plans (BIPs)

In this chapter you have learned about the reasons why students engage in challenging behaviors. You have also discovered how to define problem behaviors, gather information, and form hypotheses about environmental variables that support those behaviors. In the next chapter, we will explore ways to develop interventions based on behavior functions. The steps for defining problem responses, gathering information, forming hypotheses, and implementing BIPs are depicted in Figure 6.5.

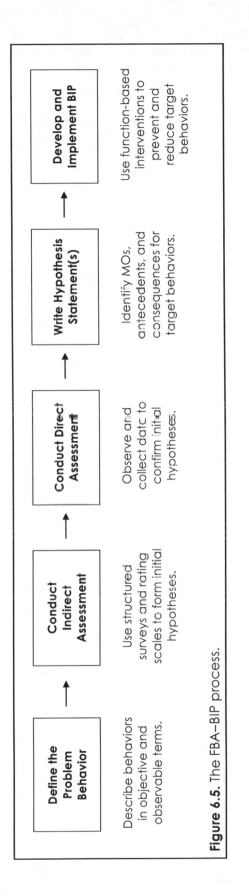

Figure 6.5. The FBA–BIP process.

Define the Problem Behavior

Describe behaviors in objective and observable terms.

Conduct Indirect Assessment

Use structured surveys and rating scales to form initial hypotheses.

Conduct Direct Assessment

Observe and collect data to confirm initial hypotheses.

Write Hypothesis Statement(s)

Identify MOs, antecedents, and consequences for target behaviors.

Develop and Implement BIP

Use function-based interventions to prevent and reduce target behaviors.

The first step is to define the problem behavior. Second, you will conduct indirect assessment to form initial hypotheses about maintaining variables. Because indirect assessment is subjective, the third step is to confirm your hypotheses through direct assessment and observation. Next, you will write hypothesis statements that describe the environmental variables maintaining the problem behavior. Finally, you will use this information to develop the student's BIP.

Summary

Functional behavioral assessment is a collection of strategies to identify the environmental reasons why students engage in challenging behaviors for the purpose of developing effective interventions. The environmental reasons for challenging behaviors are motivating operations, which alter the momentary value of reinforcers and the frequency of behaviors associated with those reinforcers; antecedents, which trigger challenging behaviors; and reinforcing consequences, including positive and negative reinforcement. There are three steps in conducting an FBA. Step 1 is to define the problem behaviors. Step 2 is to gather information through indirect and direct assessment. Step 3 is to form hypothesis statements about each problem behavior. FBA leads to the development of a function-based BIP to prevent and reduce problem behaviors.

CHAPTER 7

Function-Based Interventions and Behavior Intervention Programming

Chapter Objectives

- Describe how multicomponent interventions and contextual fit are critical in behavior intervention programming.

- Identify interventions to address motivating operations.

- Understand interventions to change antecedents.

- Describe interventions to teach alternative behaviors.

- Explain strategies to modify reinforcing consequences.

- Understand how to implement and evaluate function-based behavior intervention programming.

In this chapter, you will learn how to use information gathered in the FBA to develop function-based interventions and behavior intervention programming. First, we will discuss the importance of multicomponent interventions and contextual fit in reducing challenging behaviors. Then, we will explore interventions to address motivating operations, to change antecedents, to teach alternative behaviors, and to address consequences that reinforce problem behaviors. Finally, you will learn how these elements combine into a comprehensive behavior intervention plan.

PBS and Multicomponent Interventions

Multicomponent interventions: Simultaneously applying several interventions to prevent and eliminate problem behaviors.

You will recall from Chapter 1 that PBS involves *multicomponent interventions*, which means that several strategies are simultaneously used to prevent and eliminate problem behaviors (Carr et al., 2002). Multicomponent interventions are more likely to be successful if a particular procedure does not work because others may fill the gap to reduce targeted responses. Moreover, because the functional behavioral assessment (FBA) is likely to identify more than one controlling variable, function-based behavior intervention plans (BIPs) should employ multiple strategies to address motivating operations, antecedents, and reinforcing consequences, and to teach alternative responses.

In a review of positive behavioral intervention research targeting young children's challenging behaviors published between 1984 and 2003, Conroy, Dunlap, Clarke, and Alter (2005) noted that 45% of studies employed multicomponent interventions to successfully reduce problem behaviors. Multicomponent interventions have also been used to reduce challenging behaviors of young children and adolescents with autism (Waters, Lerman, & Hovanetz, 2009), traumatic brain injury (Feeney & Ylvisaker, 2003; Gardner, Bird, Maguire, Carreiro, & Abenaim, 2003), and adults with intellectual disabilities (Cannella, O'Reilly, & Lancioni, 2006).

PBS and Contextual Fit

Contextual fit is another important component of successful BIPs. Contextual fit refers to the compatibility of the BIP with variables in the educational environment (Albin, Luchyshyn, Horner, & Flannery,

1996). These are "(a) characteristics of the person for whom the plan is designed; (b) variables related to the people who will implement the plan; and (c) features of environments and systems within which the plan will be implemented" (p. 82). BIPs that are designed with these features in mind are more likely to work because they will have greater coherence with the student, the people who implement the BIP, and the classroom, school, or other settings that the student occupies.

> **Contextual fit:** Compatibility of the behavior intervention plan with variables in the educational environment.

The following guidelines will help you develop BIPs with good contextual fit (Tincani, 2007):

- *Seek team input.* Importantly, the BIP should be created with the input of those who will implement the plan, including teachers, teaching assistants, parents, and related services providers (e.g., speech-language pathologists). Recognize disagreement among the team and, when a particular member disagrees with one or more components, offer that member an alternative way to support the plan. Understand that everyone brings different expertise to the process. For instance, teachers and other professionals possess expert knowledge about specific behavior interventions, while parents know the student best, including his strengths and preferences.

- *Assess capacity of the team to support the BIP.* As the team selects intervention strategies, consider whether members will have the time, expertise, and necessary resources to implement the procedures with fidelity. Members may need to be trained on specific components, and some strategies may be precluded from the plan because they are resource intensive. In other cases, additional resources will need to be introduced to support interventions.

- *Assess compatibility of the BIP with schoolwide programs and administrative supports.* There are many competing demands in the school setting, including the student's participation in high-stakes testing, placement in the general education classroom, and participation in schoolwide academic and behavioral program initiatives. Consider how the BIP will be supported by, or will conflict with, competing initiatives and programs in the school. It may be beneficial for the team to create a prioritized list of interventions and implement those with higher priority first.

Next, we will discuss specific strategies to address motivating operations and antecedents, to teach alternative behaviors, and to change consequences that support problem behaviors.

Interventions to Address
Motivating Operations

As you learned in Chapter 6, motivating operations (MOs) alter the momentary value of reinforcers and the frequency of behaviors associated with those reinforcers (Laraway et al., 2003). Common examples of MOs that increase the likelihood of challenging behaviors are difficulty with the morning routine, sleep deprivation, changes in staffing, or loss of a preferred activity (see Chapter 6, p. 76). MOs are sometimes temporally distant from challenging behaviors; that is, they happen one or more hours before problem behaviors occur. This presents a challenge to intervention because you may not know that a particular MO has happened or you may not be able to alter the MO. For instance, as a teacher there is probably little that you can do to change the student's sleep patterns in the home setting.

Next, we will discuss three strategies to address MOs, which involve communicating the MO across settings, removing the MO, and neutralizing the MO.

Communicate the MO Across Settings

Once you have identified an MO that increases the likelihood of challenging behaviors, it is important to communicate the presence of the MO across settings. For example, if disruption in the morning routine increases the likelihood of a student's difficult behaviors during the school day, the teacher may arrange for the parent to communicate about the event in a home-school communication notebook. Similarly, if a fight in another classroom is likely to increase a student's problem behaviors in your classroom, you should encourage teachers to communicate the occurrence of fights or other disruptive events prior to the student's arrival in your classroom. This way, you will be prepared to intervene when the MO happens.

Remove the MO

Perhaps the most obvious way to reduce the effects of an MO is to remove it (Horner, Vaughn, Day, & Ard, 1996); however, removing the MO is only practical under certain circumstances. For example, if an unpredictable schedule increases the reinforcing value of escape-maintained problem behaviors, the teacher can change the classroom routine to make it more predictable and structured, thus making the problem behavior irrelevant for the student. Unfortunately, under many circumstances it will not be possible to eliminate the MO because it occurs in another setting (e.g., home, other classroom) or you do not have the ability to remove it (e.g., illness, loss of a preferred activity). In these cases, another alternative is to neutralize the MO.

Neutralize the MO

A *neutralizing routine* is a practical intervention to address the MO in many classroom circumstances. A neutralizing routine is an intervention to reduce the reinforcing value of a problem behavior when an MO has occurred

> **Neutralizing routine:** An intervention to reduce the reinforcing value of a problem behavior when an MO has occurred.

(Horner, Day, & Day, 1997; Sprague & Thomas, 1997). In effect, the neutralizing routine is another MO that "cancels" effects of the MO for a problem behavior. For example, if the student's loss of a preferred activity is an MO that increases the reinforcing value of challenging behaviors, we could offer the student an alternative preferred activity or give the student a choice of activities. If a traumatic event in the home setting increases the reinforcing value of difficult behaviors when the student is presented with a hard assignment, we could provide her with more assistance, make the assignment easier (e.g., fewer problems, easier problems), or provide precorrections about what she is supposed to do if she has a hard time (e.g., ask for help). Table 7.1 shows examples of MOs and neutralizing routines to counter those MOs.

Importantly, the neutralizing routine you choose should be specific to the student, the problem behavior, and the MO. Thus, the team's knowledge of the student and his preferences is critical in selecting the neutralizing routine. When an MO has occurred, be aware of specific antecedents that trigger problem behaviors. For instance, when a student has been denied a preferred activity, he may only engage in problem behaviors in the presence of a specific cue, such as when his errors are corrected (see, for example, Horner et al., 1997). In these cases, it is important to avoid delivering cues that will trigger challenging behaviors following the MO.

Interventions to Change Antecedents

The FBA is likely to identify one or more academic, social, or other environmental situations that trigger problem behaviors. Often, these antecedents can be modified to reduce or eliminate problem behaviors and to promote student skills (Butler & Luiselli, 2007; Conroy &

Activity

Identify hypothetical MOs for a student's problem behavior, and describe one strategy to neutralize each MO. Do not use one of the examples from the book.

MO: _____

_____

_____

_____

Strategy: _____

_____

_____

_____

MO: _____

_____

_____

_____

Strategy: _____

_____

_____

_____

Table 7.1
Examples of Motivating Operations and Neutralizing Routines

Motivating Operations	Neutralizing Routines
Difficulty with the morning routine (e.g., getting up late, missing the bus) Argument before school Argument in another class	Allow student extended down time or a preferred activity when he arrives in class Provide a more preferred assignment Provide more frequent breaks
Illness Sleep deprivation	Provide student with a nap if sleep deprived Allow for a choice of tasks Give more frequent breaks
Lack of attention from staff or peers Presence or absence of a specific staff person Presence or absence of a specific classmate	Give extra, noncontingent attention to the student Pair the student with an alternative, preferred staff person or student
Unpredictable schedule Disorganized transitions	Use precorrections to remind the student about upcoming events Implement an individual activity schedule Use pictures to cue the next activity
Loss of a preferred activity	Allow the student to engage in an alternative, preferred activity Provide a choice of activities

Stichter, 2003; Kern & Clemens, 2007; Luiselli, Dunn, & Pace, 2005; Stichter, Randolph, Kay, & Gage, 2009). We will explore four specific categories of antecedents and how they can be modified to prevent difficult behaviors. These involve the general environment and routine, social interaction, preferred items and activities, and nonpreferred activities and demands. Table 7.2 shows specific antecedents and strategies to eliminate those antecedents as triggers for problem behaviors.

General Environment and Routine

Examples of possible triggers involving the general environment and routine include noisy classrooms, aversive sensory stimuli (e.g., sounds, lights), unplanned disruptions in the schedule, disorganized transitions, or unstructured routines. Interventions to address these antecedents

Table 7.2
Examples of Triggering Antecedents and Interventions

Triggering Antecedents	Interventions
General environment and routine	
• Noisy classroom	• Move student to a quieter location.
• Aversive sensory stimuli (e.g., sounds, lights)	• Move student away from aversive sensory stimuli; remove stimuli.
• Unplanned schedule disruption	• Use precorrections to signal unplanned changes in routine; offer alternative, preferred activities.
• Disorganized transition	• Add signals to cue transitions; make transitions brief.
• Unstructured schedule	• Use individual and classwide activity schedules.
	• Increase consistency in the classroom schedule.
	• Increase active student responding.
Social interaction	
• Close proximity to others	• Move the student away from others.
• Close proximity to nonpreferred persons	• Pair or group the student with preferred persons.
• Crowded classroom	• Pair nonpreferred persons with preferred activities.
• Verbal interactions (e.g., voice tone, wording)	• Change wording of instructions and other verbal interactions.
	• Maintain a positive tone with student during verbal interactions.
	• Make verbal interactions concrete and direct (e.g., "What are you doing?" vs. "Please begin your assignment").
Preferred items and activities	
• Toys, games, instructional materials	• Provide an array of preferred items and activities.
	• Provide choices when preferred items and activities are not available.
	• Provide choice of preferred instructional materials.
Nonpreferred activities and demands	
• Academic and other nonpreferred assignments	• Provide a choice of assignments.
• Nonpreferred routines	• Include student interests in assignments.
	• Add preferred stimuli to assignments and routines (e.g., materials, people).
	• Decrease the difficulty of assignments.
	• Decrease work requirements.
	• Make assignments more challenging.
	• Provide more frequent breaks.
	• Alternate demanding and preferred activities.

include moving the student to a less noisy area of the room or providing an activity schedule to make the classroom routine more predictable.

Social Interaction

Social interaction triggers include the presence of a nonpreferred person (or any person) in close proximity, crowded classrooms, or staff using particular words, phrasing, or tone of voice when interacting with the student, such as when providing instructions. Possible strategies to address social interaction antecedents include changing the student's proximity to others or changing the manner in which staff verbally interact with the student (e.g., saying "I need you to start your work right now" vs. saying "It's time to begin your assignment. You have 15 minutes and then you can take a break").

Preferred Items and Activities

The presence of preferred items and activities can also evoke challenging behaviors. For instance, if another child has a toy that a student wants, he might hit the child to obtain the toy. Interventions to address preferred items and activities as triggers include providing the student with a choice of preferred items, having an array of items available, and teaching the student to make an alternative selection when a particular item is not available.

Nonpreferred Activities and Demands

Finally, nonpreferred activities and demands such as chores or academic assignments can trigger challenging behaviors. In these cases, we can modify the activity or demand in some way to make it less aversive, offer a choice of activities, or remove the demand. For instance, we could reduce the number of problems the student must complete before taking a break, allow the student to choose a partner to work with on the assignment, or offer an alternative assignment.

Teaching Alternative Behaviors

In addition to modifying MOs and antecedents, it is essential to teach alternative behaviors. *Functional communication training* (FCT) involves teaching the student an alternative, appropriate response that produces the same

> **Functional communication training (FCT):** Teaching the student an alternative, appropriate response that produces the same reinforcing consequences as the problem behavior.

Activity

Identify a hypothetical antecedent for a student's problem behavior related to the general environment and routine, social interaction, preferred items and activities, or nonpreferred activities and demands. Describe a way that you could change the antecedent so that it does not trigger the student's problem behavior. Do not use one of the examples from the book.

_____

_____

_____

_____

_____

_____

_____

_____

_____

_____

_____

_____

_____

_____

_____

_____

_____

_____

reinforcing consequences as the problem behavior. FCT makes problem behaviors irrelevant by teaching the student a better way to produce desired consequences (Carr & Durand, 1985; Dunlap, Ester, Langhans, & Fox, 2006; Durand & Carr, 1991; Durand & Merges, 2001).

FCT is a two-step process. First, FBA data are collected to identify antecedents and consequences maintaining the challenging behavior. Then, an alternative behavior that produces the same consequences is taught in situations where the problem behavior is likely to occur. For example, in their seminal study on FCT, Carr and Durand (1985) found that children's problem behaviors were more likely to occur in conditions involving low levels of adult attention and high levels of task difficulty. In these situations, children's behaviors were reinforced by attention from adults. They reduced challenging behaviors by teaching children to request adults' attention during low attention conditions or to request an adult's assistance when a difficult task was presented.

The diagrams in Figure 7.1 illustrate contingencies maintaining two problem behaviors—hitting and screaming (bottom)—and appropriate, alternative behaviors that produce the same consequences—asking for help and asking for a break (top).

You should use the following guidelines when you teach alternative responses through FCT (Durand & Merges, 2001).

- Ensure that the alternative response you teach will produce the same reinforcing consequences as the problem behavior(s).
- Chose a response modality that others are likely to recognize and reinforce. For example, a voice output communication device may not be a good choice in a noisy classroom or if staff will not always be in close proximity to the student. In these circumstances, it might be best to teach the student a highly recognizable response such as hand raising.
- Teach an alternative response that will be easier for the student to perform than the problem behavior. In general, it is best to teach a response modality that the student already knows. For instance, if the student primarily communicates by exchanging pictures, then picture exchange is probably the modality of choice.
- Provide a high level of reinforcement for the alternative response. For FCT to be successful, the alternative response must be more efficient at producing reinforcing consequences than the problem behavior. Initially, you should prompt the alternative response frequently and heavily reinforce it. As the student learns the response independently, you can thin the schedule of reinforcement to one that is reasonable for most classroom situations.

Activity

Write the contingencies maintaining a hypothetical challenging behavior in the bottom boxes, and then write an example of an appropriate, alternative behavior that produces the same reinforcing consequence in the top boxes.

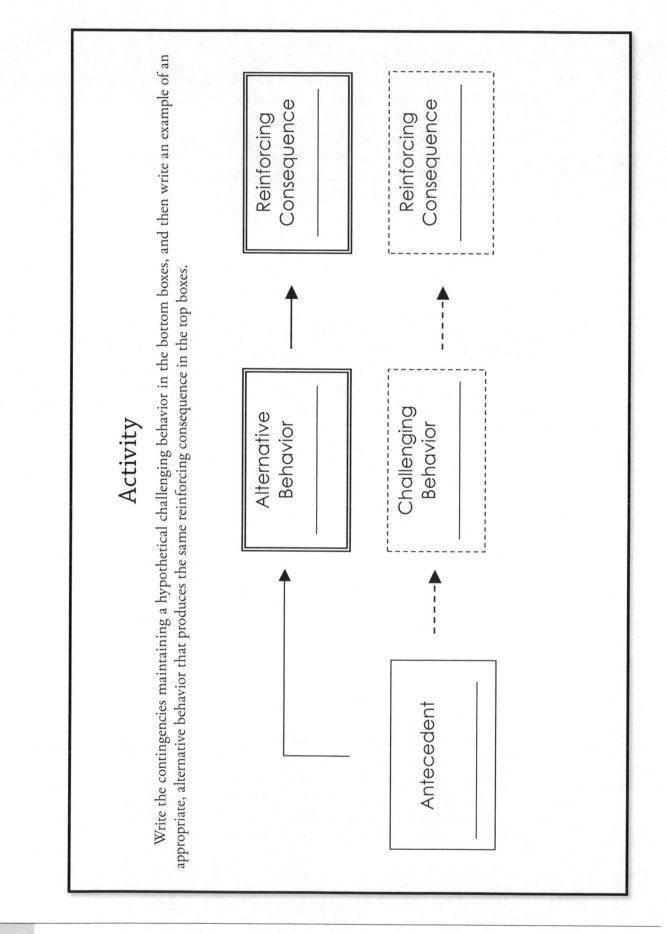

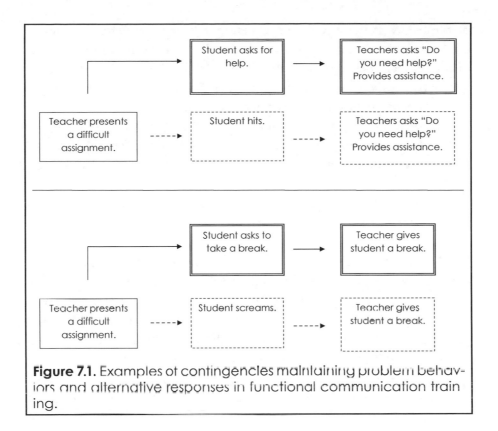

Figure 7.1. Examples of contingencies maintaining problem behaviors and alternative responses in functional communication training.

Interventions to Address Consequences

There are two categories of consequence-based interventions to reduce challenging behaviors: removing consequences for problem responses and adding consequences to support alternative responses. We will explore each.

Removing Reinforcing Consequences for Problem Responses

In Chapter 5, you learned that extinction happens when you stop delivering a reinforcer for a behavior and consequently the student performs the behavior less frequently. Thus, a basic strategy to reduce problem responses is to stop delivering consequences that reinforce them. For example, if a student engages in aggressive behavior to obtain adult attention, then you should stop delivering attention when she behaves aggressively.

However, extinction is never recommended as a stand-alone procedure to reduce problem behaviors for the following reasons. First, extinction often accompanies a phenomenon called extinction burst, that is, when you stop delivering the reinforcer, the frequency and/or intensity of the behavior initially increases before it decreases. When extinction burst occurs, it can be very difficult to withhold the reinforcer as rates of the problem behavior increase. Second, extinction does not teach any alternative responses, thus the student is likely to resume engaging in problem behaviors in situations where the reinforcer cannot be withheld. Therefore, it is always best to combine extinction with other intervention procedures, including FCT, as part of a multicomponent BIP (Fisher, Piazza, Cataldo, & Harrell, 1993; Shukla & Albin, 1996; Waters et al., 2009).

Consider the following guidelines to remove consequences for problem behaviors maintained by attention, escape, and access to preferred items.

Attention-maintained problem behaviors. Avoid making eye contact with or talking to the student following the problem behavior. Prompt the student to engage in an alternative response using the least intrusive prompt possible; gestural prompts are optimal. If you must respond to problem behaviors, remain calm, keep a neutral tone of voice, and minimize your physical interactions with the student.

Escape-maintained problem behaviors. Prompt the student to continue the activity using the least intrusive prompt (e.g., gestures). If the student is younger or has a severe intellectual disability, it may be necessary to physically block the student from escaping; if so, follow your school's or agency's procedures for physical engagement of students and only use as much physical effort as is necessary to keep the student in the activity. Provide prompts for the student to engage in alternative responses. Provide a high level of reinforcement if the student has engaged in the alternative response in the absence of problem behaviors.

Item-access-maintained problem behaviors. Block the student's access to the preferred item and minimize your verbal or physical interactions with the student. Prompt the student to engage in an alternative response (e.g., asking for the item, picking an alternative item). Provide a high level of reinforcement for alternative responses in the absence of problem behaviors.

Add Reinforcing Consequences for Appropriate Responses

As you place problem behaviors on extinction, teach alternative responses, address MOs, and change antecedents, it is critical that you add reinforcing consequences for appropriate behaviors. The basic rule is to provide behavior-specific praise, tokens, and other types of reinforcement (see Chapter 5) when the student engages in appropriate behaviors and to minimize reinforcement for problem behaviors. Remember, if you are conducting FCT, it is critically important to provide a high level of reinforcement for alternative responses at first, and then to thin the schedule of reinforcement to one that is appropriate for the classroom or other school situations.

Differential reinforcement of other behavior (DRO) is another reinforcement-based procedure to reduce challenging behaviors. DRO involves providing reinforcement to the student after he has refrained from engaging in problem behaviors for a prespecified period of time (Poling & Ryan, 1982). Presumably, the "other behavior" in DRO is anything the student is doing while not performing problem behaviors. Although DRO can be effective, a major drawback is that a student needn't be doing anything to earn the reinforcer; he simply needs to refrain from problem behaviors. Therefore, like extinction, DRO should only be used in combination with other function-based intervention strategies, including FCT, which you have learned about in this chapter.

> **Differential reinforcement of other behavior (DRO):** Providing reinforcement to the student after he has refrained from engaging in problem behaviors for a prespecified period of time.

The following are steps for implementing DRO:
- Identify the target behavior.
- Identify the reinforcer the student will earn for the DRO. If possible, involve the student in selection of the reinforcer.
- Determine the DRO interval. Typically, this is done by taking a baseline measurement of the problem behavior's frequency during a specific time period, and then dividing the frequency of the behavior by the time period. For example, if three instances of hitting are observed during a 60-minute period, and three divided by 60 is 20, then the initial DRO interval would be 20 minutes.
- Use a timer to signal the beginning of the DRO interval.
- If the student refrains from the target behavior during the entire interval, immediately provide the reinforcer.
- If the student engages in the problem behavior during the interval, you may reset the timer and allow the student another opportunity to earn the reinforcer.
- If the student is repeatedly successful in earning the reinforcer, incrementally increase the DRO interval.

Differential reinforcement of low rates of behavior (DRL), a related strategy, involves providing reinforcement if a challenging behavior occurs at or below a prespecified level during a

> **Differential reinforcement of low rates of behavior (DRL):** Providing reinforcement if a challenging behavior occurs at or below a prespecified level during a fixed time period.

fixed time period (Deitz & Repp, 1973). For example, a teacher implementing a DRL–3 procedure for talk-outs during math class would provide a reinforcer at the end of math class if the student performed three or fewer talk-outs during the class period. The reinforcer can be provided if the student engages in the behavior at or below the criterion level during an entire session, such as a math period (full session DRL), or the session can be divided into smaller intervals (e.g., 15 minutes) and the reinforcer provided if the behavior occurs at or below the criterion level during each interval (interval DRL; Deitz, 1977, 1978).

DRL is advantageous for problem behaviors that occur at a high frequency because the student is permitted to perform some of the behavior to earn reinforcement. Thus, DRL is appropriate when a low level of the behavior is tolerable. On the other hand, DRL is unlikely to eliminate the behavior entirely and should only be used when a low level of the behavior is permissible.

Follow these steps to implement DRL:

- Identify the target behavior.
- Identify the reinforcer the student will earn for the DRL. If possible, involve the student in selection of the reinforcer.
- Determine the criterion level for the DRL. This involves taking a baseline measure of the behavior, and then setting the criterion below the baseline level. For example, if the student engages in five incidents of disruptive behavior, on average, during social studies class, then the DRL criterion would be four or less (i.e., DRL–4).
- Visual cues to signal how many challenging behaviors the student has performed are helpful. Considering the previous example, the teacher can write four tally marks on the board at the beginning of the class period, and then remove a tally mark each time the student performs a disruptive behavior. If there are any tally marks remaining at the end of the class, the student has earned the reinforcer.
- If the student consistently earns the reinforcer, the DRL criterion can be incrementally reduced, or the teacher can switch to a DRO contingency.

Putting It Together: Developing a Comprehensive Behavior Intervention Plan

You have now learned how to collect data on why problem behaviors are occurring through FBA, and how to use this information to develop a function-based BIP. Figure 7.2 reviews the steps of this process. On pages 108–109 you will find a form that can be used to develop the written BIP.

Section I of the form contains spaces to write observable definitions of up to four target behaviors. Each behavior should have a name (e.g., hitting) along with an observable definition (e.g., forcefully striking another person with a hand or foot). Section II contains diagrams to write the MOs, antecedents, and consequences maintaining each problem behavior. This information is gathered from the FBA. If a particular variable is not known, then a question mark can be written in the spaces below the variable. Sections III, IV, V, and VI contain spaces to describe interventions to address MOs, to modify triggering antecedents, to teach alternative behaviors, and to address reinforcing consequences. Importantly, the procedures should be written clearly so that anyone implementing the plan can understand the plan and execute it with fidelity.

Implementing, Monitoring, and Evaluating the BIP

Once you have developed the BIP, the next step is to implement it. It is critical to make the BIP available for everyone on the team who will be responsible for executing the program. Therefore, the BIP should be publicly posted in a clear location of the classroom or included on a clipboard with the student's data sheets or other instructional materials.

An important part of implementation is monitoring the BIP to ensure that it is working. Data should be collected on each target response. Data can be collected on the frequency of target behaviors (i.e., how many times the behavior happens per period or day), rate of target behaviors (i.e., how many times the behavior happens per minute or per hour), or the duration of target behaviors (i.e., how long the target behavior occurs) before and after intervention. Data should be reviewed at least weekly to determine if the plan is reducing target behaviors, and the team should convene at least biweekly to determine if the plan needs to be changed. We will discuss using data to evaluate program outcomes in Chapter 8.

What if the plan is not working? Often, the team's BIP may not be effective in reducing target behaviors to acceptable levels or zero levels. BIPs can be unsuccessful for at least two critical reasons. First, lack

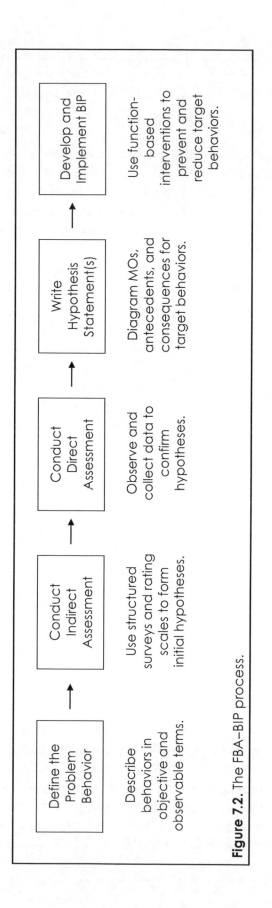

Figure 7.2. The FBA–BIP process.

Preventing Challenging Behavior in Your Classroom

of success can occur if information gathered in the FBA did not accurately identify variables maintaining the student's problem behaviors. Therefore, if the plan is not working, the team should revisit the FBA and collect additional data to verify the functions of problem behaviors, and alternative hypotheses should be considered. Second, the plan may not be working because the procedures were not implemented as intended or not implemented at all. Poor implementation can happen for a number of reasons, including lack of proper training of team members, disagreement among team members about one or more elements of the program, or lack of resources to implement the program with fidelity. If so, the team should reconvene to discuss the program and consider ways to improve implementation. Often, this involves adding procedures, omitting procedures, or adjusting procedures to meet team members' preferences or demands of the classroom or other school environments.

Summary

Function-based behavior intervention plans reduce challenging behaviors through modifying the environment according to information gathered in the functional behavioral assessment. BIPs include multicomponent interventions and should be developed with contextual fit, including input of the educational team and assessment of the team's capacity to support the program. The BIP contains interventions to address motivating operations, to change triggering antecedents, to teach alternative behaviors, and to modify reinforcing consequences. This information is summarized in a written program. Data from the BIP should be reviewed at least weekly to determine effectiveness. If the plan is not working, the team should consider collecting additional FBA data and revising initial hypotheses, and should verify that the program is being implemented as intended.

Behavior Intervention Program

Student's name: _____   Grade: _____

Person responsible for the program: _____

Date begin: _____

Review date: _____

I. Observable definitions of problem behaviors:

    a.   _____

    b.   _____

    c.   _____

    d.   _____

II. Hypotheses about variables maintaining problem behaviors (attach FBA data).

    a.   _____

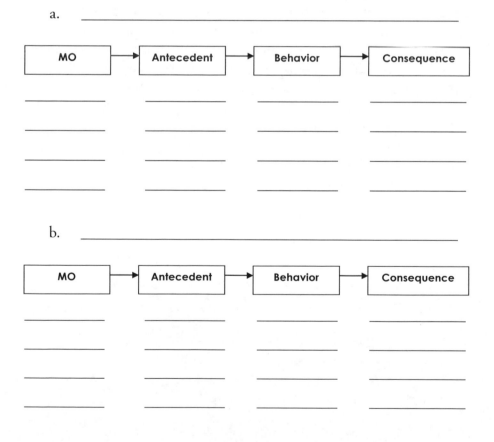

    b.   _____

c. _____

MO		Antecedent		Behavior		Consequence
	→		→		→	
_____		_____		_____		_____
_____		_____		_____		_____
_____		_____		_____		_____
_____		_____		_____		_____

d. _____

MO		Antecedent		Behavior		Consequence
	→		→		→	
_____		_____		_____		_____
_____		_____		_____		_____
_____		_____		_____		_____
_____		_____		_____		_____

III. Interventions to address motivating operations:

_____

_____

_____

_____

_____

IV. Interventions to change triggering antecedents:

_____

_____

_____

_____

_____

V. Interventions to teach functionally equivalent alternative behaviors:

_____

_____

_____

_____

_____

VI. Interventions to address reinforcing consequences:

_____

_____

_____

_____

_____

CHAPTER 8

Using Data to Evaluate PBS Outcomes

Chapter Objectives

♦ Describe why data are critical to PBS outcomes.

♦ Given a target behavior, know how to select an appropriate data collection strategy and collect data.

♦ Describe the rationale and logic of A-B designs to evaluate PBS outcomes.

♦ Understand the basic components of line graphs and how to use line graphs to evaluate data.

This chapter describes the role of data in evaluating PBS outcomes. The importance of data in PBS will be discussed, followed by an overview of data collection strategies. Then, we will learn about the role of A-B designs in program evaluation, and outline the differences between baseline and intervention conditions. Finally, we will summarize the basic components of line graphs and learn how to construct graphs for program assessment.

Why Are Data Important?

Suppose that you have implemented an individualized PBS program to reduce a student's challenging behaviors and increase her appropriate behaviors. How will you know that the program is working? A commonly employed strategy to evaluate behavior interventions is an informal one: You might think about differences between the student's behaviors before and after the intervention, or ask someone else, "How is she doing since we started the program?" Your estimation of how well the student is doing will be influenced by your history with her, the opportunities you have to observer her (or lack thereof), and your opinions about her skills and severity of her challenging behaviors. In other words, the resulting information will be subjective. Therefore, because informal evaluation is unlikely to yield accurate and reliable information about the student's progress, it is not a useful strategy to evaluate PBS programming.

Data: Objective information about a behavior that enables a teacher to make informed decisions about PBS programming.

Data-based decision making: The ongoing process of using data to determine how well the student is doing and to make program changes accordingly.

A better approach involves the systematic use of data to assess program outcomes. *Data* are objective information about a behavior that enable a teacher to make informed decisions about PBS programming. *Data-based decision making* is the ongoing process of using data to determine how well the student is doing and to make program changes accordingly. Importantly, the data we collect have no value unless we actively use them to evaluate and change the student's program according to his progress.

Accountability is another important reason to collect data. For example, for children with disabilities, the Individualized Education Program (IEP) team will convene at least annually to review the students' progress in attaining special education program goals and objectives. Data provide a systematic means to evaluate IEP outcomes and to hold team members accountable for their respective roles. Conversely, absence of data may lead to questions about students' progress and the overall quality and appropriateness of special education programs.

Collecting Data

The data collection strategy you choose will be determined by key characteristics of your student's target behaviors. We will focus on six strategies: event recording, rate recording, duration recording, latency recording, interval recording, and momentary time sampling. An overview of the five data collection strategies, characteristics of behaviors that are appropriate for each strategy, and examples of behaviors that are appropriate for each strategy is presented in Table 8.1.

Event Recording

Event recording involves recording each time the student performs a behavior, and then adding the tally marks to yield a frequency of the behavior per class period, session, or day. For example, Campbell and Lutzker (1993) used event recording to measure the impact of functional communication training (see

> **Event recording:** Tallying each time the student performs a behavior, and then adding the tally marks to yield a frequency of the behavior per class period, session, or day.

Chapter 7) on throwing and destroying items, screaming, and sign language use of Don, a boy with autism. Event recording is most appropriate for behaviors that are discrete—that is, they have a definite beginning and end—and do not occur at such a high frequency that it is practically impossible to count them. For instance, event recording would not be appropriate for a student who engages in self-stimulatory rocking hundreds of times during the class period. Event recording is also not an appropriate strategy for behaviors that occur for longer time periods (e.g., silent reading); for these behaviors, duration recording is most appropriate (see below). Event recording is a useful strategy for behaviors that leave a permanent product that can be counted. For instance, spelling words correctly written on a worksheet or envelopes correctly labeled can be tallied to yield a frequency count.

Figure 8.1 shows a sample event recording data sheet for a student, James. The two rows contain hypothetical data for two behaviors, talking-out and hand-raising. The observer, Ms. Watkins, has tallied the frequency of each behavior during one-hour observation periods throughout the day. At the end of the day, she adds the tally marks to determine the total frequency of the target behaviors.

Table 8.1
Overview of Data Collection Strategies

Strategy	Procedure	Appropriate for	Examples
Event recording	Record each time the student performs a behavior	• Discrete behaviors • Behaviors that leave a permanent product that can be counted	• Hand raising • Hitting • Writing numbers
Rate recording	Record each time the student performs a behavior, divide frequency of behavior by unit of time	• Behaviors for which speed + accuracy is important • Observation periods that are variable in duration	• Typing on a keyboard • Oral reading • Assembling packages
Duration recording	Record the amount of time the student engages in a behavior	• Behaviors where time is an important dimension • Behaviors that have a definite beginning and end	• Silently reading • Playing with peers • Crying
Latency recording	Record the time period between an instructional cue and when the student performs a behavior	• Situations in which the student takes a long time to respond to a cue or instructions	• Responding to teacher directions • Leaving the building after a fire alarm • Exiting the classroom after the bell
Interval recording	Divide an observation period into equal intervals, and then record whether the behavior has occurred during each interval	• Behaviors that do not have a definite beginning or end • High-rate behaviors • Multiple behaviors or multiple students	• Self-stimulatory behavior • On-task behavior • Disruptive behavior
Momentary time sampling	Divide an observation period into equal intervals, and then record whether the behavior is occurring at the end of each interval	• Same as interval recording	• Same as interval recording

Preventing Challenging Behavior in Your Classroom

	8:00-9:00	9:00-10:00	10:00-11:00	11:00-12:00	12:00-1:00	1:00-2:00	2:00-3:00	3:00-4:00	TOTAL

Student(s): James — M (T) W R F   Date 1/27

Observer: Ms. Watkins

(Behavior)/ Student: Talking-out

| | II | ⅢⅢ | ○ | ○ | III | I | ○ | ○ | 11 |

(Behavior)/ Student: Hand-raising

| | II I | III | I | I I | I | ○ | I I | I | 13 |

Figure 8.1 Sample event recording data sheet.

The same form can be used to event record the behaviors of multiple students. In each row labeled "Behavior / Student," you can write the name of a student and the student's behavior that you are recording (e.g., teasing—Colin). Then, you can make tally marks for each student's behavior in the spaces below. A blank event recording form is found in Figure 8.2.

Rate Recording

Rate recording is a variation of event recording that is appropriate when you are concerned with how quickly and accurately the student performs a behavior. Rate recording is also appropriate when the duration of your observation periods is variable. Like event recording, rate recording involves tallying each time the student performs a behavior and then adding the tally marks to yield a frequency of the behavior per class period, session, or day. However, with rate recording, you then divide the total frequency of behavior by a unit of time (e.g., minutes, hours).

> **Rate recording:** A variation of event recording in which the total frequency of a behavior is divided by a unit of time (e.g., minutes, hours).

For certain behaviors, such as reading orally, writing answers to multiplication facts, or typing on a keyboard, you will be concerned with how quickly, as well as how accurately, the student performs the behavior. For instance, you might want a student to orally read 100 words per minute, write correct answers to 20 multiplication facts per minute, or type 120 words per minute. Rate recording is appropriate for such behaviors. The formula for calculating the rate of behavior is:

$$\frac{\text{Frequency of behavior}}{\text{Time}} = \text{Rate}$$

For example:

$$\frac{\text{42 answers correct}}{\text{2 minutes}} = \text{21 answers correct per minute}$$

Rate recording is also useful when you are collecting data on the frequency of a behavior, as in event recording, but the duration of your observation periods is variable. Consider the hypothetical data below:

Day	Monday	Tuesday	Wednesday	Thursday	Friday
Observation period	1 hour	1.5 hours	2 hours	1 hour	1.5 hours
Frequency	27	29	36	22	32
Rate per hour	27	19.3	18	22	21.3

If we look at the third row, which represents the frequency of behaviors, the behavior occurred at its highest frequency on Wednesday, 36, and at its lowest frequency on Thursday, 22. However, the duration of the observation periods—that is, the amount of time the student had opportunity to perform the behavior—skews our frequency counts; shorter observation periods yield lower frequencies, while longer observation periods yield higher frequencies. For a more accurate measure of the behavior, we should convert the frequency to rate. Looking at the fourth row, rate per hour, we can see that the behavior occurred at its highest rate on Monday, 27, and at its lowest rate on Wednesday, 18. When observation periods are variable, it is necessary to convert frequency data to rate to yield the most accurate picture of the behavior.

Duration Recording

Duration recording: Recording the amount of time the student engages in a behavior.

There are certain behaviors for which time is the most important dimension. Consider a student who has lengthy tantrums lasting up to 45 minutes. Event recording will probably

Student(s):				M T W R F	Date:				
Observer:									
									TOTAL
Behavior / Student:									
Behavior / Student:									
Behavior / Stucent:									
Behavior / Stucent:									
Behavior / Stucent:									
Behavior / Stucent:									
Behavior / Stucent:									

Figure 8.2. Blank event recording data sheet.

not yield an accurate picture of these behaviors, particularly if tantrums occur only once or twice per day. Instead, we should use *duration recording*, in which we record the amount of time the student engages in a behavior. Crozier and Tincani (2007) used duration recording to determine if Social Stories™ increased the amount of time that Thomas, a preschool student, sat during circle time. Other behaviors appropriate for duration recording include time spent working on homework, crying, or time out-of-seat.

Duration recording is only appropriate if you can determine when a behavior starts and stops. To conduct duration recording, the observer carries a stopwatch, smart phone, or other device equipped with a stopwatch application. When the behavior begins, the stopwatch is started; when the behavior stops, the stopwatch is paused. Data can be collected on the total duration of the behavior during an observation period, or the total duration can be divided by the frequency of the behavior to yield an average duration of the behavior per observation period.

Figure 8.3 contains a sample duration data recording form. Ms. Alvarez has recorded the duration of two behaviors, out-of-seat and tantrums. In each space under the cells labeled, "Obs.," she records the start and stop time for each behavioral episode. Then, in the space labeled, "Total," she writes the total duration of all of the behaviors during the observation. Finally, in the space labeled "Average," she writes the average duration of all of the behaviors, which is determined by dividing the frequency of behaviors by the total duration. Figure 8.4 contains a blank data sheet that can be used for duration recording.

Latency Recording

Latency recording: Recording the time period between an instructional cue and when the student performs a behavior.

Like duration recording, *latency recording* involves time as a unit of measurement. However, in latency recording, we measure the time period between an instructional cue and when the student performs a behavior. Latency recording is often used when we wish to reduce the amount of time it takes for a student to begin a task or comply with instructions. For example, Heinicke, Carr, and Mozzoni (2009) used latency recording to evaluate the effects of rules and a token economy on reducing the amount of time it took for Claire, an adolescent girl with acquired brain injury, to comply with academic instructions. Other behaviors where latency recording is useful include time to transition from one activity to another or time required to exit the school building following an alarm during a fire drill.

Activity

Below are a set of hypothetical data representing number of words orally read per minute. In the row labeled rate per minute, calculate the rate of behavior for each day by dividing the frequency of behavior by unit of time (minutes). Space is provided below for your calculations, if needed.

Day	Monday	Tuesday	Wednesday	Thursday	Friday
Observation period	2 minutes	4 minutes	3 minutes	4 minutes	2 minutes
Frequency	220	484	290	442	248
Rate per minute					

The data sheet shown in Figure 8.4 can also be used for latency recording as well. Instead of recording the duration of each behavior, the teacher would start the stopwatch when an instructional cue is given, and then stop the stopwatch when the student performs the behavior. As with duration recording, the latencies can be summed and then divided by the number of behaviors to yield an average latency for each observation period.

Interval Recording

Interval recording: Dividing an observation period into equal intervals and then recording whether the behavior occurs during each interval.

Partial-interval recording: A type of interval recording in which the behavior is recorded if it occurs during any part of the interval.

Whole-interval recording: A type of interval recording in which the behavior is recorded if it occurs during the entire interval.

Our next data collection strategy, *interval recording*, involves dividing an observation period into equal intervals and then recording whether the behavior occurs during each interval. There are two variations of interval recording. In *partial-interval recording*, we record if the behavior occurs during **any part** of the interval; in *whole-interval recording*, we record if the behavior occurs during the **entire** interval.

Interval recording is the preferred data collection strategy under three conditions. First, if it is difficult for observers to tell when the behavior starts and stops, interval recording is useful because it does not require the observer to note the beginning or end of behaviors. Interval recording is also a good strategy for very high-rate behaviors that cannot be tallied with event or rate recording. Finally, interval recording is useful when recording multiple behaviors or the behaviors of multiple students. Although interval recording is advantageous in these situations, a substantial limitation of interval recording versus event, rate, duration, and latency recording is that it provides only an indirect measure of the behavior. Therefore, interval recording should only be used with behaviors for which the other recording systems are inappropriate.

The two variations of interval recording, partial-interval recording and whole-interval recording, are prescribed under different circumstances. Partial-interval recording tends to overestimate the occurrence of a behavior, and therefore is used to measure challenging behaviors that we want to reduce. For example, Haley, Heick, and Luiselli (2010) used partial-interval recording to measure the effects of antecedent cue cards on reducing the vocal stereotypy (e.g., repetitive sounds, humming) of Sean, an 8-year-old boy with autism.

Student(s): _Rayna_

Observer: _Ms. Alvarez_

M T W (TH) F   Date: _4/28_

Behavior/ Student: Out-of-seat

Obs. 1	Obs. 2	Obs. 3	Obs. 4	Obs. 5	Obs. 6	Obs. 7	Obs. 8	Total	Average
:00 /:42	:43 / 1:28	1:29 / 2:36	2:37 / 3:01	3:02 / 3:31	3:32 / 4:02	4:03 / 4:47	4:48 / 5:02	5:02	38 s.

Behavior/ Student: Tantrum

Obs. 1	Obs. 2	Obs. 3	Obs. 4	Obs. 5	Obs. 6	Obs. 7	Obs. 8	Total	Average
:00 / 5:24	5:25 / 10:17	10:18/ 15:21	__/__	__/__	__/__	__/__	__/__	15:21	5 m. 12 s.

Figure 8.3. Sample duration data recording form.

Student(s): _____   M T W TH F   Date: _____

Observer: _____

Behavior / Student:											
Behavior / Student:											
Behavior / Student:											
Behavior / Student:											
Behavior / Student:											
Behavior / Student:											
Behavior / Student:											
Behavior / Student:											

Figure 8.4. Blank form for recording duration data.

Whole-interval recording, in contrast, tends to underestimate the occurrence of behavior, and is often used when we are trying to measure academic, social, communicative, or other behaviors that we want to increase. Graham-Day, Gardner, and Hsin (2010) collected data with whole-interval recording to assess the effects of self-monitoring and reinforcement on the on-task behaviors of three 10th-grade students with Attention Deficit/Hyperactivity Disorder (ADHD).

Figure 8.5 shows a hypothetical interval recording data sheet for Madison. Mr. Chen is measuring Madison's rocking and repetitive vocalizations using partial-interval recording. The observation period, which lasts for 5 minutes, has been divided into 30-second intervals. Mr. Chen makes a plus mark if the behavior occurs during any part of the interval; he makes a zero mark if the behavior does not occur during any part of the interval. The resulting data can be converted to a percentage of intervals; therefore, Madison engaged in rocking for 40% of intervals and repetitive vocalizations for 30% of intervals during the 5-minute observation period.

Interval recording is a useful strategy when you are attempting to record several behaviors simultaneously or the behaviors of several students simultaneously. Figure 8.6 shows a partial-interval recording data sheet for three students to measure three behaviors—hitting, screaming, and asking. The data sheet represents a rotating observation system; the observer records the behavior of Student 1 during the first interval, Student 2 during the second interval, Student 3 during the third interval, and so on. The rotating observation system results in fewer intervals of data; however, it enables the scorer to capture data on more behaviors than would be possible with a continuous recording system.

Our final data collection strategy, *momentary time sampling*, is like interval recording in that we divide our observation period into equal intervals. However, the observer records only whether the behavior is occurring at the **end** of each interval (i.e., at the moment each interval is ending). Typically, the end of the interval is cued by a repeating signal (e.g., beep from a timer) that tells the observer when to record. The primary advantage of momentary time sampling is that it does not require the recorder to continually observe behaviors. This is a significant practical advantage in classroom situations where the teacher must simultaneously deliver instruction and collect data. Momentary time sampling also enables the observer to collect data of several students and several behaviors at the same time.

> **Momentary time sampling:** Dividing an observation period into equal intervals, and then recording whether the behavior is occurring at the end of each interval.

Student(s): __Madison__

Observer: __Mr. Chen__

M T W TH (F)   Date: __5/5__

Behavior / Student: Rocking									
:00–:30	:30–1:00	1:00–1:30	1:30–2:00	2:00–2:30	2:30–3:00	3:00–3:30	3:30–4:00	4:00–4:30	4:30–5:00
+	o	+	+	o	o	o	o	o	+

Behavior / Student: Repetitive vocalizations (humming, yelling)									
:00–:30	:30–1:00	1:00–1:30	1:30–2:00	2:00–2:30	2:30–3:00	3:00–3:30	3:30–4:00	4:00–4:30	4:30–5:00
o	o	o	+	+	o	o	o	o	+

Figure 8.5. Sample interval recording data sheet.

Student(s): _____ M T W TH F   Date:_____

Observer: _____

| A = Asking | S = Screaming | H = Hitting |

Interval	Time	Student 1	Student 2	Student 3
1	:10	(H) S A	H S A	H S A
2	:20	H S A	H S (A)	H S A
3	:30	H S A	H S A	(H) (S) A
4	:40	H S (A)	H S A	H S A
5	:50	H S A	(H) S A	H S A
6	1:00	H S A	H S A	H (S) (A)
7	1:10	H S (A)	H S A	II S A
8	1:20	H S A	H S A	H S A
9	1:30	H S A	H S A	H (S) A
10	1:40	H S A	H S A	H S A
11	1:50	H S A	H S (A)	H S A
12	2:00	H S A	H S A	H (S) A
13	2:10	H (S) A	H S A	H S A
14	2:20	H S (A)	H (S) A	H S A
15	2:30	H S A	H S A	H (S) A
16	2:40	H (S) A	H S A	H S A
17	2:50	H S A	(H) (S) A	H S A
18	3:00	H S A	H S A	H S (A)
19	3:10	H (S) A	H S A	H S A
20	3:20	H S A	H S (A)	H S A
21	3:30	H S A	H S A	H (S) A
22	3:40	H (S) (A)	H S A	H S A
23	3:50	H S A	H S A	H S A
24	4:00	H S A	H S A	H S (A)
25	4:10	H (S) A	H S A	H S A
26	4:20	H S A	H S (A)	H (S) A
27	4:30	H S A	H S A	H S A
28	4:40	H S A	H S A	H S A
29	4:50	H S A	(H) S A	H S A

Figure 8.6. Sample partial-interval recording data sheet.

Activity

In the spaces below, describe a student's hypothetical academic, social, or challenging behavior that you wish to measure. Identify which of the six data collection systems is most appropriate to measure the behavior and why. Discuss any practical constraints that affected your selection of the data collection system.

_____

_____

_____

_____

_____

_____

_____

_____

_____

_____

_____

_____

_____

_____

_____

_____

_____

_____

_____

A disadvantage of momentary time sampling is that it provides the least direct measure of behaviors and tends to overestimate or underestimate behaviors. Inaccuracies are more likely with longer intervals (i.e., one minute or greater; Rapp, Colby-Dirksen, Michalski, Carroll, & Lindenberg, 2008). The data sheets in Figure 8.4 can also be used for momentary time sampling.

A-B Designs to Evaluate PBS Outcomes

Once you have selected a data collection system, your next step is to collect and graph your data. Remember, the primary reason for collecting data is to evaluate PBS programming and make any needed changes to the intervention. Therefore, you want to collect data frequently to provide an accurate picture of the student's progress. For some behaviors, you should collect data on a daily basis; for others, collecting data 2–3 times per week or once per week will be sufficient. Data should be reviewed at least weekly to assess students' progress with PBS programming.

A-B designs provide a means to evaluate the relationship between a behavior and your intervention. A-B designs is a type of single-subject design that compares a person's behavior under a baseline condition with no intervention (A) to a second condition, in which an intervention is applied (B). A-B designs employ baseline logic (Bailey & Burch, 2002), which is illustrated by Figure 8.7.

> **A-B design:** A single-subject design that compares a person's behavior under a baseline condition with no intervention (A) to a second condition, in which an intervention is applied (B)

The top panel of Figure 8.7 shows a graph for hitting with five baseline data points (left). The dotted lines show the range of the data points. If the teacher continued to collect data for additional days, do you think the behavior would improve? It would probably not. The dotted lines on the right side of the graph indicate that the behavior would likely continue at its baseline level if no intervention was applied.

In contrast, the bottom panel shows a graph in which an intervention was applied to reduce hitting. Visual inspection of the graph shows that the behavior was reduced below its baseline level during the intervention; therefore, we can conclude that the intervention was successful in reducing the student's hitting below its baseline level.

How long should you collect baseline data before implementing your intervention? Typically, a minimum of 3–5 data points are necessary; however, as illustrated in Figure 8.7, your baseline data should be stable enough (or trending in a worsening direction) for you to predict that the behavior would not improve without intervention.

Graphing Data

Five essential components should be included on every behavior graph. The graph in Figure 8.8 shows the effects of an intervention involving functional communication training, precorrections, and a token economy on the duration of a student's tantrums. The critical elements are:

a.   *Y-axis.* Shows the behavior's level and has a descriptive label that describes the behavior and how it was measured (e.g., total duration of hitting).

b.   *X-axis.* Depicts the passage of time and shows the unit measurement (e.g., school days, class periods, hourly sessions).

c.   *Data path.* Data points represent the level of behavior for each observation period with lines to connect the data points.

d.   *Condition labels.* Describes the condition that was in effect during data collection. Interventions are briefly described.

e.   *Condition change line.* Indicates the change of one condition (e.g., baseline) to another (e.g., intervention). The data points on either side of the condition line are not connected.

Importantly, you should graph your data frequently to assess your student's progress with the program. It is best to graph your data points daily or as often as you collect data.

What if the program is not working? Your graph may show that the student's behavior remains at baseline level after you implement the intervention. As we learned in Chapter 7, interventions can fail for a number of reasons, including the failure of interventions to address the functions of challenging behaviors and lack of implementation fidelity. In some cases, it will be necessary to change interventions or add interventions in order to reduce problem behaviors to acceptable levels. Figure 8.9 shows a graph depicting the effects of two interventions on percentage of intervals of disruption. The first intervention, response cards, failed to reduce disruption below its baseline level. Therefore, the teacher had to add a second intervention—or C condition—the good behavior game, which reduced disruption to acceptable levels.

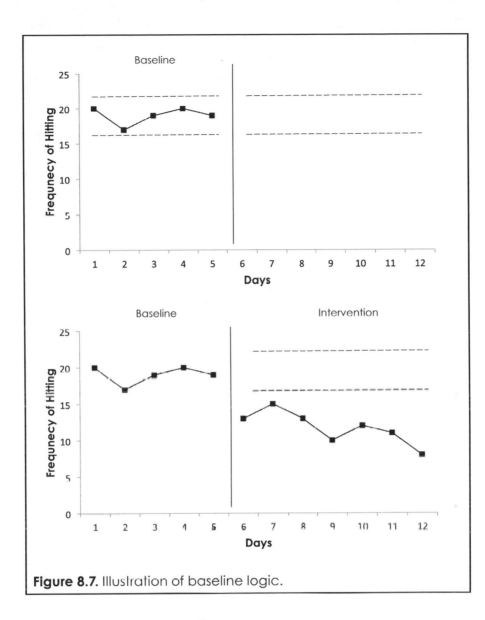

Figure 8.7. Illustration of baseline logic.

Summary

Data are necessary to evaluate PBS programming and to hold team members accountable for their respective roles. Your data collection system—event, rate, duration, latency, interval recording, or momentary time sampling—should be selected according to key characteristics of the behavior(s) you wish to measure. Data on target behaviors should be collected frequently and evaluated on at least a weekly basis. A-B designs permit you to compare your student's performance before and after intervention. Graphs contain essential information about a student's performance and allow you to visually assess his or her progress and make program changes accordingly.

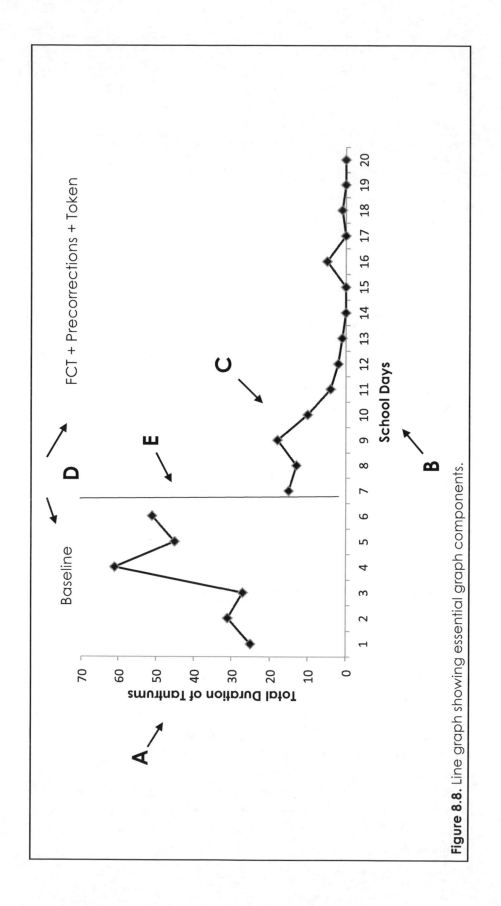

Figure 8.8. Line graph showing essential graph components.

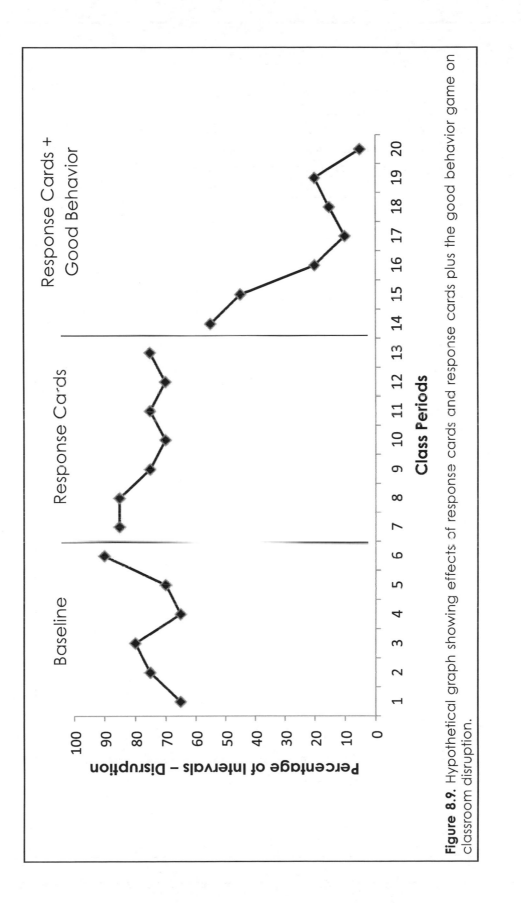

Figure 8.9. Hypothetical graph showing effects of response cards and response cards plus the good behavior game on classroom disruption.

Activity

In the empty space below, draw a line graph showing the effects of an intervention on a hypothetical student's challenging behavior. The graph should show baseline and intervention conditions and should contain the five essential elements described above—the Y axis, X axis, condition, data path, condition labels, and condition change line(s).

Preventing Challenging Behavior in Your Classroom

Putting It Together: The Reflective Classroom Manager Survey

In this book you have learned about many strategies for reducing your students' challenging behaviors and increasing their appropriate behaviors through positive behavior support. The Reflective Classroom Management Survey below summarizes key areas of classroom management covered in the book and provides a means for you to evaluate and improve your performance in these areas. If you are currently teaching, complete the survey to develop an action plan for improving your classroom management skills. If you are not currently teaching, once you have your own classroom you can complete the survey to reflect on your future classroom management skills and identify key areas for improvement.

The survey is divided into two sections. Part I allows you to evaluate your performance for each classroom management skill we have covered in the book. Part II enables you to select the classroom management area for which you need the most improvement and to develop an action plan to increase your skill in one to three specific skills. Repeat the survey as often as needed to reflect on your classroom management performance.

Reflective Classroom Manager Survey

Teacher's Name: _____   **Date:** _____

Grade/Subject: _____   **School:** _____

Instructions:

Part I: For the key components of classroom management below, circle 1–5 to indicate the extent to which each is in place in your classroom:

- 1 = totally not in place,
- 2 = mostly not in place,
- 3 = partially in place,
- 4 = mostly in place, and
- 5 = totally in place or not applicable.

Then, determine the average score for each classroom management area by adding the total score and dividing by the total possible score, as shown in the boxes.

Part II: For the classroom management area with the *lowest average score*, select one to three key components for improvement. For example, if Classroom-Wide Behavior Support receives your lowest score, you might select contingent praise and attention, classroom rules, or active supervision for improvement. Then, in the following spaces, describe your action plan for improving your performance on the three components (e.g., I will seek student input to create a set of classroom rules, post them, and develop a lesson plan for teaching them). Then, identify a time for your achieving and evaluating your improvement plan.

Revisit the survey as often as necessary to reflect on your classroom management performance and to target key areas for improvement.

Part I

	In place?
Classroom Organization (Chapter 3)	
Student schedules (pp. 28–33)	
Demanding and preferred activities are alternated	1 2 3 4 5
Long activities are broken up into shorter activities, as appropriate	1 2 3 4 5
Choices are offered	1 2 3 4 5
Whole class schedule is posted	1 2 3 4 5
Individual student schedules are in place, as appropriate	1 2 3 4 5
Physical Space (pp. 34–35)	
Classroom is neat	1 2 3 4 5
Instructional areas are clearly defined	1 2 3 4 5
Seating is arranged according to activities and students' needs	1 2 3 4 5
Seating is arranged to minimize student distractions	1 2 3 4 5
Physical space is arranged to accommodate students with limited mobility	1 2 3 4 5
Transitions (pp. 35–37)	
Activity transitions are brief	1 2 3 4 5
End of activities is signaled by a clear cue	1 2 3 4 5
All lesson preparation is completed before lessons begin	1 2 3 4 5
Working With Teaching Assistants (pp. 37–38)	
Performance expectations are explicit	1 2 3 4 5
Ongoing feedback is provided	1 2 3 4 5
Classroom Organization Average	_____ / 75 = _____
Active Student Responding (Chapter 4)	
Response cards are used to promote ASR (pp. 41–44)	1 2 3 4 5
Choral responding is used to promote ASR (p. 45)	1 2 3 4 5
Guided notes are used to promote ASR (pp. 45–47)	1 2 3 4 5
Brisk instructional pacing is used (pp. 46–50)	
Lessons are organized	1 2 3 4 5
Wait-time is minimized, as appropriate	1 2 3 4 5
Intertrial intervals are minimized	1 2 3 4 5
Feedback is immediately provided	1 2 3 4 5
Active Student Responding Average	_____ / 40 = _____
Classroom-Wide Behavior Support (Chapter 5)	
Contingent praise and attention is delivered at a 4:1 ratio (pp. 56–58)	1 2 3 4 5
Behavior-specific praise is delivered (pp. 58–59)	1 2 3 4 5

Students are taught to appropriately recruit teacher attention (pp. 60–61)	1 2 3 4 5
Errors are systematically corrected (pp. 61–63)	1 2 3 4 5
Classroom rules are posed and rule following is reinforced (pp. 63–65)	1 2 3 4 5
Group contingencies are in place (pp. 65–69)	1 2 3 4 5
Active supervision is occurring (p. 70)	1 2 3 4 5
Classroom-Wide Behavior Support Average	_____ / 35 = _____
FBA and Function-Based Interventions (Chapters 6–7)	
Functional behavioral assessments are conducted for students with chronic challenging behaviors (pp. 73–88)	1 2 3 4 5
Function-based behavior intervention plans are implemented for students with chronic challenging behaviors (pp. 89–110)	1 2 3 4 5
FBA and Function-Based Interventions Average	_____ / 10 = _____
Data Collection (Chapter 8)	
Data on challenging and appropriate behaviors are collected on an ongoing basis (pp. 112–125)	1 2 3 4 5
Data are converted in graphs and reviewed on at least a weekly basis	1 2 3 4 5
Data are used to make changes to student programming	1 2 3 4 5
Data Collection Average	_____ / 15 = _____

Part II

1. Classroom management area with <u>lowest average score</u>:

    _____

2. One to three key areas for improvement:

    a. _____

    b. _____

    c. _____

3. Action plan for improvement:

    _____

    _____

    _____

    _____

    _____

    _____

    _____

    _____

    _____

    _____

    _____

    _____

    _____

    _____

    _____

4. I will complete and evaluate my action plan by (exact date):

    _____

Glossary

A-B Design: A single-subject design that compares a person's behavior under a baseline condition with no intervention (A) to a second condition, in which an intervention is applied (B).

Active student responding: When a student emits a detectable response to ongoing instruction, such as saying, writing, or typing an answer.

Active supervision: When the teacher actively looks around the classroom, moves around the classroom, and interacts with students to prevent instances of problem behaviors.

Alterable variables: Things the teacher can change to produce improvements in students' learning and behaviors. These include the pace of teaching, responses to problem behaviors, and choice of materials.

Antecedents: Stimuli that trigger challenging behaviors.

Applied behavior analysis (ABA): Application of the science of behavior analysis to improve socially significant behaviors. ABA emphasizes continuous measurement, close examination of the student's environment, and manipulation of antecedents and consequences to accomplish behavior change.

Behavior intervention plan (BIP): A written plan that describes procedures to prevent and reduce a student's challenging behaviors and how data will be used to evaluate these procedures. BIPs are designed for students who display chronic or intense challenging behaviors.

Behavior-specific praise: Praise that provides information about the type, quality, or level of a student's behaviors.

Brisk instructional pacing: When the teacher moves quickly through the lesson's content, minimizing down time, while giving students sufficient wait-time to answer questions.

Choice making: Providing students with an opportunity to make limited and reasonable choices in the context of classroom routines to promote self-determination and prosocial behaviors.

Choral responding: When students vocally respond in unison to teacher-presented questions.

Classroom-wide token systems: A type of independent group contingency in which the teacher makes the delivery of a reward contingent on each student earning a specified number of tokens, which are then exchanged for a back-up reward.

Contextual fit: Compatibility of the behavior intervention plan with variables in the educational environment.

Contingent praise and attention: The application of praise and other forms of attention only when the student has performed specific academic, social, or other good behaviors.

Data: Objective information about a behavior that enables a teacher to make informed decisions about PBS programming.

Data-based decision making: The ongoing process of using data to determine how well the student is doing and to make program changes accordingly.

Dependent group contingencies: A type of group contingency in which students earn rewards as a group contingent upon some or all of the group's behavior.

Differential reinforcement of low rates of behavior (DRL): Providing reinforcement if a challenging behavior occurs at or below a prespecified level during a fixed time period.

Differential reinforcement of other behavior (DRO): Providing reinforcement to the student after he has refrained from engaging in problem behaviors for a prespecified period of time.

Direct assessment: Observing the student in settings where problem behaviors occur and collecting data to discover patterns between antecedents, behaviors, and consequences.

Duration recording: Recording the amount of time the student engages in a behavior.

Error correction: When a teacher systematically responds to an error to increase the student's accuracy with a skill.

Event recording: Tallying each time the student performs a behavior, and then adding the tally marks to yield a frequency of the behavior per class period, session, or day.

Extinction: When you stop delivering a reinforcer for a behavior and consequently the student performs the behavior less frequently.

Extinction burst: When you stop delivering a reinforcer for a behavior and the frequency and/or intensity of a behavior initially increases before it decreases.

Formal indirect assessments: Questionnaires and rating scales to systematically identify behavior functions.

Functional analysis: Experimental manipulation of variables thought to maintain challenging behaviors for the purpose of identifying behavior functions.

Functional behavioral assessment (FBA): A collection of strategies to identify the environmental reasons why students engage in challenging behaviors for the purpose of developing effective interventions. These include indirect assessments, direct assessments, and functional analysis.

Functional communication training (FCT): Teaching the student an alternative, appropriate response that produces the same reinforcing consequences as the problem behavior.

Good behavior game: A type of dependent group contingency in which the class is divided into two teams who compete for a reward based upon which team displays the fewest problem behaviors.

Group contingencies: Special reinforcement systems in which part or all of the class must perform appropriate behaviors to earn a reward.

Guided notes: Handouts for lectures that allow students to write the key facts, concepts, and/or relationships being discussed in prepared spaces.

Independent group contingencies: A type of group contingency in which each student earns rewards for her own behaviors.

Indirect assessment: Interviewing people who know the student to gather information about variables maintaining problem behaviors.

Individual student schedule: A personalized written or pictorial schedule that lists the activities a student is supposed to do throughout the school day.

Individualized Education Program (IEP): A written plan that describes how a student's special education program will be delivered and evaluated. Required components include present levels of performance, measurable goals and objectives, related services and accommodations, and how the child's progress will be documented.

Inter-trial interval: The time period between the teacher's feedback and the next teacher-posed question.

Interval recording: Dividing an observation period into equal intervals, and then recording whether the behavior occurs during each interval.

Latency recording: Recording the time period between an instructional cue and when the student performs a behavior.

Momentary time sampling: Dividing an observation period into equal intervals and then recording whether the behavior is occurring at the end of each interval.

Motivating operations (MOs): Events that alter the momentary value of reinforcers and the frequency of behaviors associated with those reinforcers.

Multicomponent interventions: Simultaneously applying several interventions to prevent and eliminate problem behaviors.

Negative reinforcement: When you remove something following a behavior that increases the likelihood that the behavior will occur again.

Neutralizing routine: An intervention to reduce the reinforcing value of a problem behavior when an MO has occurred.

Nonalterable variables: Things that affect students' learning and behaviors that are beyond the teacher's control (e.g., disabilities, genes, poverty).

Partial-interval recording: A type of interval recording in which the behavior is recorded if it occurs during any part of the interval.

Positive behavior support (PBS): An approach to prevent and reduce challenging behavior through comprehensive lifestyle changes, a lifespan perspective, stakeholder participation, socially valid interventions, systems change, multicomponent interventions, prevention, flexibility with respect to scientific practices, and multiple theoretical perspectives.

Positive reinforcement: When you add something following a behavior that increases the likelihood that the behavior will occur again.

Precorrections: Reminders for students to engage in appropriate behaviors and to refrain from inappropriate behaviors.

Punishment: Any event following a behavior that decreases the likelihood that the behavior will occur in the future.

Rate recording: A variation of event recording in which the total frequency of a behavior is divided by a unit of time (e.g., minutes, hours).

Reinforcement: Any event following a behavior that increases the likelihood that the behavior will occur again.

Response cards: Blank or preprinted cards on which students write or select answers during teacher-directed lessons.

Response to Intervention (RtI): A multitiered approach that emphasizes prevention of academic failure through early screening and intervention.

Teaching students to recruit teacher attention: Instructions, prompts, and reinforcement to help students to independently get the teacher's attention when they have completed their work or need help from the teacher to complete their work.

Thinning the schedule of reinforcement: The process of gradually decreasing how frequently you deliver reinforcement (e.g., praise, rewards) to a student. This can be accomplished by increasing the number of responses required to earn reinforcement or by increasing the amount of time with appropriate behavior that must pass before the student earns reinforcement.

Wait-time: The interval between when the teacher asks a question and the student responds, usually controlled by a cue from the teacher.

Whole-class schedule: A publicly posted schedule that depicts what the entire class is doing throughout the school day.

Whole-interval recording: A type of interval recording in which the behavior is recorded if it occurs during the entire interval.

References

Alber, S., & Heward, W. (1997). Recruit it or lose it!: Training students to recruit positive teacher attention. *Intervention in School and Clinic, 32,* 275–282.

Alber, S., Heward, W., & Hippler, B. (1999). Teaching middle school students with learning disabilities to recruit positive teacher attention. *Exceptional Children, 65,* 253–270.

Alberto, P. A., & Troutman, A. C. (2009). *Applied behavior analysis for teachers* (8th ed.). Upper Saddle River, NJ: Pearson.

Albin, R. W., Luchyshyn, J. M., Horner, R. H., & Flannery, K. B. (1996). Contextual fit for behavioral support plans: A model for "goodness of fit." In L. Koegel, R. Koegel, & G. Dunlap (Eds.), *Positive behavioral support: Including people with difficult behavior in the community* (pp. 81–98). Baltimore, MD: Brookes.

Bailey, J. S., & Burch, M. R. (2002). *Research methods in applied behavior analysis.* Thousand Oaks, CA: Sage.

Barbetta, P., Heron, T., & Heward, W. (1993). Effects of active student response during error correction on the acquisition, maintenance, and generalization of sight words by students with developmental disabilities. *Journal of Applied Behavior Analysis, 26,* 111–119.

Barbetta, P., & Heward, W. (1993). Effects of active student response during error correction on the acquisition and maintenance of geography facts by elementary students with learning disabilities. *Journal of Behavioral Education, 3,* 217–233.

Barrish, H., Saunders, M., & Wolf, M. (1969). Good behavior game: Effects of individual contingencies for group consequences on disruptive behavior in a classroom. *Journal of Applied Behavior Analysis, 2,* 119–124.

Bayat, M., Mindes, G., & Covitt, S. (2010). What does RTI (Response to Intervention) look like in preschool? *Early Childhood Education Journal, 37,* 493–500.

Bijou, S. W., Peterson, R. F., & Ault, M. H. (1968). A method to integrate descriptive and experimental field studies at the level of data and empirical concept. *Journal of Applied Behavior Analysis, 1,* 175–191.

Bloom, B. S. (1980). The new direction in educational research: Alterable variables. *Phi Delta Kappan, 61,* 382–385.

Butler, L., & Luiselli, J. (2007). Escape-maintained problem behavior in a child with autism: Antecedent functional analysis and intervention evaluation of noncontingent escape and instructional fading. *Journal of Positive Behavior Interventions, 9,* 195–202

Cameron, J., & Pierce, W. (1994). Reinforcement, reward, and intrinsic motivation: A meta-analysis. *Review of Educational Research, 64,* 363–423.

Campbell, R. V., & Lutzker, J. R. (1993). Using functional equivalence training to reduce severe challenging behavior: A case study. *Journal of Developmental and Physical Disabilities, 5,* 203–216.

Cannella, H., O'Reilly, M., & Lancioni, G. (2006). Treatment of hand mouthing in individuals with severe to profound developmental disabilities: A review of the literature. *Research in Developmental Disabilities, 2,* 529–544.

Carnine, D. W. (1976). Effects of two teacher-presentation rates on off-task behavior, answering correctly, and participation. *Journal of Applied Behavior Analysis, 9,* 199–206

Carr, E. G., Dunlap, G., Horner, R. H., Koegel, R. L., Turnbull, A. P., Sailor, W., . . . Fox, L. (2002). Positive behavior support: Evolution of an applied science. *Journal of Positive Behavior Interventions, 4,* 4–16, 20.

Carr, E. G., & Durand, V. M. (1985). Reducing problem behaviors through functional communication training. *Journal of Applied Behavior Analysis, 18,* 111–126.

Carter, D., & Horner, R. (2007). Adding functional behavioral assessment to first step to success: A case study. *Journal of Positive Behavior Interventions, 9,* 229–238.

Carter, D., & Horner, R. (2009). Adding function-based behavioral support to first step to success: Integrating individualized and manualized practices. *Journal of Positive Behavior Interventions, 11,* 22–34.

Clunies-Ross, P., Little, E., & Kienhuis, M. (2008). Self-reported and actual use of proactive and reactive classroom management strategies and their relationship with teacher stress and student behaviour. *Educational Psychology, 28,* 693–710.

Colvin, G., Sugai, G., Good, R., & Lee, Y. (1997). Using active supervision and precorrection to improve transition behaviors in an elementary school. *School Psychology Quarterly, 12,* 344–363.

Conroy, M., Dunlap, G., Clarke, S., & Alter, P. (2005). A descriptive analysis of positive behavioral intervention research with young children with challenging behavior. *Topics in Early Childhood Special Education, 25,* 157–166.

Conroy, M., & Stichter, J. (2003). The application of antecedents in the functional assessment process: Existing research, issues, and recommendations. *The Journal of Special Education, 37,* 15–25.

Conroy, M., Sutherland, K., Snyder, A., & Marsh, S. (2008). Classwide interventions: Effective instruction makes a difference. *TEACHING Exceptional Children, 40,* 24–30.

Cooper, J. O., Heron, T. E., & Heward, W. L. (2007). *Applied behavior analysis* (2nd ed.). Upper Saddle River, NJ: Pearson.

Craft, M., Alber, S., & Heward, W. (1998). Teaching elementary students with developmental disabilities to recruit teacher attention in a general education classroom: Effects on teacher praise and academic productivity. *Journal of Applied Behavior Analysis, 31,* 399–415.

Crozier, S., & Tincani, M. (2007). Effects of social stories on prosocial behavior of preschool children with autism spectrum disorders. *Journal of Autism and Developmental Disorders, 37,* 1803–1814.

De Pry, R. L., & Sugai, G. (2002). The effect of active supervision and pre-correction on minor behavioral incidents in a sixth grade general education classroom. *Journal of Behavioral* Education, *11,* 255–264.

Deitz, S. M. (1977). An analysis of programming DRL schedules in educational settings. *Behaviour Research and Therapy, 15,* 103–111.

Deitz, S. M. (1978). Reducing inappropriate behavior in special classrooms by reinforcing average interresponse times: Interval DRL. *Behavior Therapy, 9,* 37–46.

Deitz, S. M. & Repp, A. C. (1973). Decreasing classroom misbehavior through the use of DRL schedules of reinforcement. *Journal of Applied Behavior Analysis, 6,* 457–463.

Dolan, L., Kellam, S., Brown, C., & Werthamer-Larsson, L. (1993). The short-term impact of two classroom-based preventive interventions on aggressive and shy behaviors and poor achievement. *Journal of Applied Developmental Psychology, 14,* 317–345.

Duncan, A. (2009, October). *Teacher preparation: Reforming the uncertain profession.* Remarks at Teachers College, Columbia University

Dunlap, G., Carr, E., Horner, R., Zarcone, J., & Schwartz, I. (2008). Positive behavior support and applied behavior analysis: A familial alliance. *Behavior Modification, 32,* 682–698.

Dunlap, G., Ester, T., Langhans, S., & Fox, L. (2006). Functional communication training with toddlers in home environments. *Journal of Early Intervention, 28,* 81–96.

Dunlap, G., & Fox, L. (1999). A demonstration of positive behavioral support for young children with autism. *Journal of Positive Behavioral Interventions, 1,* 77–87.

Durand, V. M., & Carr, E. G. (1991). Functional communication training to reduce challenging behavior: Maintenance and application in new settings. *Journal of Applied Behavior Analysis, 24,* 251–264.

Durand, V. M., & Crimmins, D. B. (1988). *The Motivation Assessment Scale.* Topeka, KS: Monaco & Associates.

Durand, V. M., & Merges, E. (2001). Functional communication training: A contemporary behavior analytic intervention for problem behavior. *Focus on Autism and Other Developmental Disabilities, 16,* 110–119.

Ellis, J., & Magee, S. (1999). Determination of environmental correlates of disruptive classroom behavior: Integration of functional analysis into public school assessment process. *Education & Treatment of Children, 22,* 291–316.

Feeney, T., & Ylvisaker, M. (2003). Context-sensitive behavioral supports for young children with TBI: Short-term effects and long-term outcome. *The Journal of Head Trauma Rehabilitation, 18,* 33–51.

Fisher, W., Piazza, C., Cataldo, M., & Harrell, R. (1993). Functional communication training with and without extinction and punishment. *Journal of Applied Behavior Analysis, 26,* 23–36.

Fuchs, D., & Deshler, D. (2007). What we need to know about responsiveness to intervention (and shouldn't be afraid to ask). *Learning Disabilities Research & Practice, 22,* 129–136.

Fuchs, D., & Fuchs, L. (2008). Implementing RTI. *District Administration, 44,* 72–76.

Gardner, R., Bird, F., Maguire, H., Carreiro, R., & Abenaim, N. (2003). Intensive positive behavior supports for adolescents with acquired brain injury: Long-term outcomes in community settings. *The Journal of Head Trauma Rehabilitation, 18,* 52–74.

Godfrey, S., Grisham-Brown, J., Schuster, J., & Hemmeter, M.L. (2003). The effects of three active responding techniques on student participation and social behavior with preschool children with special needs. *Education and Treatment of Children, 26,* 255–272.

Graham-Day, K. J., Gardner, R., & Hsin, Y. (2010). Increasing on-task behaviors of high school students with Attention Deficit Hyperactivity Disorder: Is it enough? *Education & Treatment of Children, 33,* 205–221.

Greenwood, C., Hops, H., Delquadri, J., & Guild, J. (1974). Group contingencies for group consequences in classroom management: A further analysis. *Journal of Applied Behavior Analysis, 7,* 413–425.

Greenwood, C. R., Delquadri, J., & Hall, R. V. (1984). Opportunity to respond and student academic achievement. In W. L. Heward, T. E. Heron, D. S. Hill, & J. Trap-Porter (Eds.), *Focus on behavior analysis in education* (pp. 58–88). Columbus, OH: Merrill.

Grskovic, J., & Belfiore, P. (1996). Improving the spelling performance of students with disabilities. *Journal of Behavioral Education, 6,* 343–354.

Haley, J. L., Heick, P. F., & Luiselli, J. K. (2010). Use of an antecedent intervention to decrease vocal stereotypy of a student with autism in the general education classroom. *Child & Family Behavior Therapy, 32,* 311–321.

Hall, L., McClannahan, L., & Krantz, P. (1995). Promoting independence in integrated classrooms by teaching aides to use activity schedules and decreased prompts. *Education & Training in Mental Retardation & Developmental Disabilities, 30,* 208–217.

Hall, R. V., Lund, D., & Jackson, D. (1968). Effects of teacher attention on study behavior. *Journal of Applied Behavior Analysis, 1,* 1–12.

Harris, V., & Sherman, J. (1973). Use and analysis of the "good behavior game" to reduce disruptive classroom behavior. *Journal of Applied Behavior Analysis, 6,* 405–417.

Haydon, T., Mancil, G., & Van Loan, C. (2009). Using opportunities to respond in a general education classroom: A case study. *Education & Treatment of Children, 32,* 267–278.

Heinicke, M. R., Carr, J. E., & Mozzoni, M. P. (2009). Using differential reinforcement to decrease academic response latencies of an adolescent with acquired brain injury. *Journal of Applied Behavior Analysis, 42,* 861–865.

Heron, T. E., & Harris, K. C. (2001). *The educational consultant.* Austin, TX: Pro-Ed.

Heron, T. E., Hippler, B., & Tincani, M. (2003). *How to help students complete classwork and homework assignments.* Austin, TX: Pro-Ed.

Heward, W. L. (1994). Three low-tech strategies for increasing the frequency of active student response during group instruction. In R. Gardner, III, D. Sainato, J. O. Cooper, T. Heron, W. L. Heward, J. Eshleman, & T. A. Grossi (Eds.), *Behavior analysis in education: Focus on measurable superior instruction* (pp. 283–320). Pacific Grove, CA: Brooks/Cole.

Heward, W. L. (2003). Ten faculty notions about teaching and learning that hinder the effectiveness of special education. *The Journal of Special Education, 36,* 186–205.

Horner, R., Day, H., & Day, J. (1997). Using neutralizing routines to reduce problem behaviors. *Journal of Applied Behavior Analysis, 30,* 601–614.

Horner, R., Dunlap, G., Koegel, R., & Carr, E. (1990). Toward a technology of "nonaversive" behavioral support. *Journal of the Association for Persons With Severe Handicaps, 15,* 125–132.

Horner, R., Sugai, G., Smolkowski, K., Eber, L., Nakasato, J., Todd, A., & Esperanza, J. (2009). A randomized, wait-list controlled effectiveness trial assessing school-wide positive behavior support in elementary schools. *Journal of Positive Behavior Interventions, 11,* 133–144.

Horner, R. H., Vaughn, B. J., Day, H. M., & Ard, W. R. (1996). The relationship between setting events and problem behavior: Expanding our understanding of behavioral support. In L. K. Koegel, R. L. Koegel, & G. Dunlap (Eds.), *Positive behavioral support: Including people with difficult behavior in the community* (pp. 381–402). Baltimore, MD: Brookes.

Hulac, D. M., & Benson, N. (2010). The use of group contingencies for preventing and managing disruptive behaviors. *Intervention in School and Clinic, 45,* 257–262.

Individuals with Disabilities Education Improvement Act, Pub. Law 108-446 (December 3, 2004).

Iwata, B. A., & DeLeon, I. G. (2005). *The functional analysis screening tool (FAST).* Gainesville: University of Florida, The Florida Center on Self-Injury.

Iwata, B. A., Dorsey, M., Slifer, K., Bauman, K., & Richman, G. (1994). Towards a functional analysis of self-injury. *Journal of Applied Behavior Analysis, 27,* 197–209. [Reprinted from *Analysis and Intervention in Developmental Disabilities, 2,* 3–20.]

Johnson, T., Stoner, G., & Green, S. (1996). Demonstrating the experimenting society model with classwide behavior management interventions. *School Psychology Review, 25,* 199–214.

Johnson-Gros, K., Lyons, E., & Griffin, R. (2008). Active supervision: An intervention to reduce high school tardiness. *Education & Treatment of Children, 31,* 39–53.

Keiper, R., & Busselle, K. (1996). The rural educator and stress. *Rural Educator, 17,* 18–21.

Kern, L., & Clemens, N. (2007). Antecedent strategies to promote appropriate classroom behavior. *Psychology in the Schools, 44,* 65–75.

Kohn, A. (1993). *Punished by rewards: The trouble with gold stars, incentive plans, A's, praise, and other bribes.* Boston, MA: Houghton Mifflin.

Kokkinos, C. (2007). Job stressors, personality and burnout in primary school teachers. *British Journal of Educational Psychology, 77,* 229–243.

Konrad, M., Joseph, L., & Eveleigh, E. (2009). Meta-analytic review of guided notes. *Education & Treatment of Children, 32,* 421–444.

Lalli, J., Pinter-Lalli, E., Mace, F., & Murphy, D. (1991). Training interactional behaviors of adults with developmental disabilities: A systematic replication and extension. *Journal of Applied Behavior Analysis, 24,* 167–174.

Lambert, M., Cartledge, G., Heward, W., & Lo, Y. (2006). Effects of response cards on disruptive behavior and academic responding during math lessons by fourth-grade urban students. *Journal of Positive Behavior Interventions, 8,* 88–99.

Laraway, S., Snycerski, S., Michael, J., & Poling, A. (2003). Motivating operations and terms to describe them: Some further refinements. *Journal of Applied Behavior Analysis, 36,* 407–414.

Lee, D. L., & Axelrod, S. (2005). *Behavior modification: Basic principles.* Austin, TX: Pro-Ed.

Lewis, R. (1999). Teachers coping with the stress of classroom discipline. *Social Psychology of Education, 3,* 155–171.

Lovaas, I. O. (1987). Behavioral treatment and normal educational and intellectual functioning in young autistic children. *Journal of Consulting and Clinical Psychology, 55,* 3–9.

Luiselli, J., Dunn, E., & Pace, G. (2005). Antecedent assessment and intervention to reduce physical restraint (protective holding) of children and adolescents with acquired brain injury. *Behavioral Interventions, 20,* 51–65.

Maag, J. (2001). Rewarded by punishment: Reflections on the disuse of positive reinforcement in schools. *Exceptional Children, 67,* 173–186.

Maheady, L., Sacca, M. K., & Harper, G. F. (1987). Classwide student tutoring teams: The effects of peer-mediated instruction on the academic performance of secondary mainstreamed students. *Journal of Special Education, 21,* 107–121.

March, R. E., Horner, R. H., Lewis-Palmer, T., Brown, D., Crone, D., Todd, A. W., & Carr, E. G. (2000). *Functional Assessment Checklist: Teachers and Staff (FACTS)*. Eugene, OR: Educational and Community Supports.

Massey, N., & Wheeler, J. (2000). Acquisition and generalization of activity schedules and their effects on task engagement in a young child with autism in an inclusive pre–school classroom. *Education & Training in Mental Retardation & Developmental Disabilities, 35,* 326–335.

Matson, J. L., & Vollmer, T. (1995). *Questions About Behavioral Function (QABF)*. Baton Rouge, LA: Disability Consultants.

Morrison, T. (1979). Classroom structure, work involvement, and social climate in elementary school classrooms. *Journal of Educational Psychology, 71,* 471–477.

National Center for Education Statistics. (1999). *Teacher quality: A report on the preparation and qualifications of public school teachers.* Washington, DC: U.S. Department of Education.

National Center for Education Statistics. (2000). *Schools and staffing survey (SASS), "Public teacher questionnaire," 1993–94 and 1999–2000.* Washington, DC: U.S. Department of Education.

O'Neill, R. E., Horner, R. H., Albin, R. W., Sprague, J. R., Storey, K., & Newton, J. S. (1997). *Functional assessment and program development for problem behavior: A practical handbook* (2nd ed.). Pacific Grove, CA: Brooks/Cole.

O'Reilly, M., Sigafoos, J., Lancioni, G., Edrisinha, C., & Andrews, A. (2005). An examination of the effects of a classroom activity schedule on levels of self-injury and engagement for a child with severe autism. *Journal of Autism and Developmental Disorders, 35,* 305–311.

Poling, A., & Ryan, C. (1982). Differential-reinforcement-of-other-behavior schedules: Therapeutic applications. *Behavior Modification, 6,* 3–21.

Rapp, J. T., Colby-Dirksen, A. M., Michalski, D. N., Carroll, R. A., & Lindenberg, A. M. (2008). Detecting changes in simulated events using partial-interval recording and momentary time sampling. *Behavioral Interventions, 23,* 237–269.

Ray, K., & Watson, T. (2001). Analysis of the effects of temporally distant events on school behavior. *School Psychology Quarterly, 16,* 324–342.

Rosenfield, P., Lambert, N., & Black, A. (1985). Desk arrangement effects on pupil classroom behavior. *Journal of Educational Psychology, 77,* 101–108.

Scott, T., Anderson, C., & Spaulding, S. (2008). Strategies for developing and carrying out functional assessment and behavior intervention planning. *Preventing School Failure, 52,* 39–49.

Shukla, S., & Albin, R. (1996). Effects of extinction alone and extinction plus functional communication training on covariation of problem behaviors. *Journal of Applied Behavior Analysis, 29,* 565–568.

Simonsen, B., Fairbanks, S., Briesch, A., Myers, D., & Sugai, G. (2008). Evidence-based practices in classroom management: Considerations for research to practice. *Education & Treatment of Children, 31,* 351–380.

Skinner, B. F. (1953). *Science and human behavior.* New York, NY: Macmillan.

Skinner, C., Williams, R., & Neddenriep, C. (2004). Using interdependent group-oriented reinforcement to enhance academic performance in general education classrooms. *School Psychology Review, 33,* 384–397.

Snider, V. E. (2006). *Myths and misconceptions of teaching: What really happens in the classroom.* Lanham, MD: Rowman & Littlefield Education.

Sprague, J., & Thomas, T. (1997). The effect of a neutralizing routine on problem behavior performance. *Journal of Behavioral Education, 7,* 325–334.

Spriggs, A., Gast, D., & Ayres, K. (2007). Using picture activity schedule books to increase on-schedule and on-task behaviors. *Education and Training in Developmental Disabilities, 42,* 209–223.

Stage, S., & Quiroz, D. (1997). A meta-analysis of interventions to decrease disruptive classroom behavior in public education settings. *School Psychology Review, 26,* 333–368.

Stichter, J., Randolph, J., Kay, D., & Gage, N. (2009). The use of structural analysis to develop antecedent-based interventions for students with autism. *Journal of Autism and Developmental Disorders, 39,* 883–896.

Sugai, G. (2007). Prompting behavioral competence in schools: A commentary on exemplary practices. *Psychology in the Schools, 44,* 113–118.

Sugai, G. (2008, August). *Is PBIS evidence-based?* Presentation to the Illinois Leadership Forum, Rosemont, IL. Retrieved from http://www.pbis.org/common/pbisresources/presentations/0808sgpbisevidencebased_IL.ppt

Sugai, G., & Horner, R. (2002). The evolution of discipline practices: School-wide positive behavior supports. *Child & Family Behavior Therapy, 24,* 23–50.

Sugai, G., & Horner, R. (2008). What we know and need to know about preventing problem behavior in schools. *Exceptionality, 16,* 67–77.

Sutherland, K., Wehby, J., & Copeland, S. (2000). Effect of varying rates of behavior-specific praise on the on-task behavior of students with EBD. *Journal of Emotional and Behavioral Disorders, 8,* 2–8, 26.

Tincani, M. (2007). Beyond consumer advocacy: Autism spectrum disorders, effective instruction, and public schooling. *Intervention in School and Clinic, 43,* 47–51.

Tincani, M., Castrogiavanni, A., & Axelrod, S. (1999). A comparison of the effectiveness of brief versus traditional functional analyses. *Research in Developmental Disabilities, 20,* 327–338.

Tincani, M., & Crozier, S. (2007). Comparing brief and extended wait-time during small group instruction for children with challenging behavior. *Journal of Behavioral Education, 16,* 355–367.

Tincani, M., Ernsbarger, S. C., Harrison, T. J., & Heward, W. L. (2005). The effects of fast and slow-paced teaching on participation, accuracy, and off-task behavior of children in the Language for Learning program. *Journal of Direct Instruction, 5,* 97–109.

Touchette, P. E., MacDonald, R. F., & Langer, S. N. (1985). A scatter plot for identifying stimulus control of challenging behavior. *Journal of Applied Behavior Analysis, 18,* 343–351.

Trussell, R. P. (2008). Classroom universals to prevent problem behaviors. *Intervention in School and Clinic, 43,* 179–185.

Wannarka, R., & Ruhl, K. (2008). Seating arrangements that promote positive academic and behavioural outcomes: A review of empirical research. *Support for Learning, 23,* 89–93.

Waters, M., Lerman, D., & Hovanetz, A. (2009). Separate and combined effects of visual schedules and extinction plus differential reinforcement on problem behavior occasioned by transitions. *Journal of Applied Behavior Analysis, 42,* 309–313.

Wood, W., Fowler, C., Uphold, N., & Test, D. (2005). A review of self-determination interventions with individuals with severe disabilities. *Research and Practice for Persons With Severe Disabilities, 30,* 121–146.

Xin, Y., Grasso, E., Dipipi-Hoy, C., & Jitendra, A. (2005). The effects of purchasing skill instruction for individuals with developmental disabilities: A meta-analysis. *Exceptional Children, 71,* 379–400.

About the Author

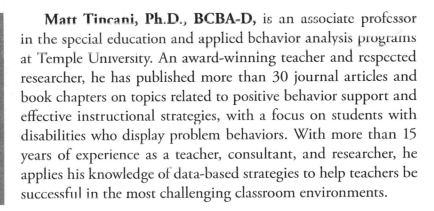

Matt Tincani, Ph.D., BCBA-D, is an associate professor in the special education and applied behavior analysis programs at Temple University. An award-winning teacher and respected researcher, he has published more than 30 journal articles and book chapters on topics related to positive behavior support and effective instructional strategies, with a focus on students with disabilities who display problem behaviors. With more than 15 years of experience as a teacher, consultant, and researcher, he applies his knowledge of data-based strategies to help teachers be successful in the most challenging classroom environments.